TEXTBOOK OF
PRACTICAL PSYCHOLOGY

TEXTBOOK OF PRACTICAL PSYCHOLOGY

By

CHARLES FOX

AKANSHA PUBLISHING HOUSE
NEW DELHI-110 059 (INDIA)

AKANSHA PUBLISHING HOUSE
R-37B, Vani Vihar, Uttam Nagar,
New Delhi-110059

Showroom
4649/21B, Ansari Road
Daryaganj, New Delhi - 110 002
PHones: 23263193, 9811582579

Textbook of Practical Psychology
Reprint. 2023

PRINTED IN INDIA

PREFACE

THE content of a course of practical educational psychology is still a matter of debate, and this book is intended as a partial solution of the problem. The course of work here presented has been given for some years to students of Education in Cambridge University. It is hoped that it may have a wider appeal, since although the material has a definite educational bias, it ought to be of use to others who are interested in the practical psychology of the higher mental processes from other standpoints.

The subject-matter has been made as concrete and as little artificial as possible, consistently with a scientific treatment, so that apparatus is reduced to a minimum and all of it can be home made. All the exercises are quantitative, as the course is meant for class use, and qualitative work can be performed by individuals at their leisure. Many of the experiments are original, whilst the others have been modified to fit in with the scheme, and a technique has been developed to suit the exigencies of class work. One of the great difficulties of practical work in this subject is the accurate recording and evaluation of the data, and it is hardly an exaggeration to say that unless this is done experimental psychology is apt to be a waste of time. For this reason much attention has been given to devising schemata for recording observations, including introspective data. With the same end in view a discussion of the results is appended to most of the experiments.

An integral part of a course in practical educational psychology is the manipulation of statistical tables, for which reason Part II is wholly concerned with this branch of the subject. Exercises have been selected as far as possible from material having an educational bearing, and the examples are mostly drawn from actual researches instead of being invented for the purpose. The student cannot too soon be introduced to the actual tables he will come across in his subsequent reading.

Every writer on statistics owes a debt to the writings of Galton, Pearson, and Yule, and I gratefully acknowledge my indebtedness. I desire also to record my thanks to my pupil Mr. H. R. King for help in the selection of material for Experiment 24; to my colleague Mr. F. E. E. Harvey for the selection of the records in Experiment 25; to my pupil Mr. E. R. Clarke for his great care in checking the working of the exercises in Part II; and to the Editor of the *British Journal of Psychology* for permission to use the illustrations and material in Appendix I from an article of mine in vol. xv. of that Journal.

CHARLES FOX.

WARKWORTH HOUSE,
CAMBRIDGE.

CONTENTS

CHAPTER XIII

CHAPTER XIV

CHAPTER XV

CHAPTER XVI

APPENDICES

INTRODUCTION

THE following instructions should be carefully read prior to the beginning of the experimental work. The course is intended for group work in a laboratory or class room, and each experiment takes approximately two hours to perform, if carried out in the manner prescribed. At the beginning of the term the class should be divided up into subjects and experimenters, who choose each other so as to be able to work together for the whole session. In several of the experiments each person acts as subject and experimenter in turn, whilst in a few cases the demonstrator is the sole experimenter for the whole group. It is important that the choice of partners should be carefully made in order that they may get into *rapport* with each other as early as possible.

The technique of the experiments has been carefully elaborated for the purposes of group work and tested over a prolonged period in the laboratory. Obvious changes have been rejected for sufficient reasons; and consequently no departure from the instructions should be made except when it is suggested in the text. The student must remember that a psychological experiment is a delicate affair, so that slight deviations in procedure which may appear unimportant are nevertheless bound to make a difference in the result. If observations are to be used for comparative purposes pedantic accuracy of technique is absolutely essential. An apparently minute variation in stimulus may make an unexpected and profound difference in the response. In a psychological experiment there is no such thing as a stimulus of a purely objective nature; since every stimulus is a stimulus to some person. The mental make-up of the person determines the kind of response just as much as the objective nature of the stimulus. The student of practical psychology must get into the habit of regarding the stimulus as an incentive or prompting to activity rather than the sole determinant of the activity.

Before any experiment begins the experimenter must make himself familiar with the instructions in the text. He should have ready in his note-book the scheme for recording observations which he will find in the text, leaving plenty of space for taking down the introspections of the subject. An essential part of every psychological experiment is the record of such introspections. Without them, *pace* the behaviourists, there is no psychological record. Both the subject and the experimenter should enter up the results of the same experiment in their respective note-books. When the experiment is complete and the necessary calculations have been made, the discussion of results to be found in the text should be carefully read and compared with the observations made in the laboratory. Any serious divergence should be accounted for in the note-books. As the discussions in the text are based on the experiments themselves conducted in the manner described in the book they indicate the degree of accuracy which should be attained in the readings. If the order of accuracy is lower than this there has usually been something wrong in carrying out the instructions.

In recording the experiments, which are all quantitative, it must be borne in mind that qualitative and more especially introspective observations are at least as important as numerical results, and should be carefully noted down. A sharp distinction must be made between actual observations and inferences therefrom. This is almost impossible with beginners, as the subject himself is as likely as not to give an inference in place of an introspective observation. Moreover, the experimenter, though he may not be a beginner, is especially likely to fall into the 'psychologist's fallacy' of confusing his own standpoint with that of the person about whom he is making a record. He supposes, that is, that the subject responds to a stimulus or an instruction in the same way in which he himself would respond. In fact, he is apt to regard himself as 'normal' and deviations from himself as needing explanation (see James' *Principles of Psychology*, vol. i., p. 196).

The above blunder is most likely to occur in experiments dealing with mental imagery; and in fact is repeatedly made. The experimenter must carefully avoid the delusive supposition that the mode of presentation (visual, auditory, etc.) necessarily determines the kind of imagery that will be evoked by the subject, or that his own imagery is the 'natural' one. There is no *a priori* reason why a visual stimulus, for instance, should arouse a visual image rather than any other kind; and the supposition that when a subject sees a picture, and thereafter remembers it, he must see it in his mind's eye, though specious, is faulty.

There are several excellent manuals dealing with mental tests and containing the better known varieties. A course in practical psychology ought to prepare the student for evaluating such tests from the inside, as it were. The best way of doing this is to undergo similar tests oneself, and the type of reasoning tests, etc., given in the book may help the person to realise sympathetically the sort of difficulty a child meets in coping with a test which is up to the limits of his capacity. In addition to the tests in the book it is advisable for the class to work one of the better known series of group tests with a time limit. For this purpose Series No. 33 issued by the National Institute of Industrial Psychology is admirable.

The statistical part of the book is intended to be worked concurrently with the experimental portion. It is based largely on the contingency table, the structure of which must be thoroughly grasped before any progress can be made. Several examples of such tables are given in the text from published researches, and others should be sought and examined in order that the general relation between the variables may be seen on inspection. The idea underlying such tables is very simple and the student should get into the habit of arranging observations in this form. Where the laboratory work provides numerical data for them, as in Experiments 24 and 25, they should be constructed by all the members of the class.

The calculation of the various coefficients is a laborious arithmetical process, but the terrors of this can be eliminated if the class works as a group. For this purpose each pair of students should take a single 'array,' the one checking the other's arithmetic. The means, deviations and other values are then pooled by the demonstrator who writes them up on the board, whence they are copied into the note-books, and the final calculations are made by the whole class. By this means the most imposing table is easily tackled and the calculations checked in a very short time. With some such division of labour it is possible for all the statistical exercises to be done by all the class as a regular part of the course of practical work.

Note-books with squared paper on alternate pages are the most convenient to use and they should contain both the experimental records and the worked statistical exercises. They are best written up at home since the two hours assigned to the experiments is usually insufficient for careful entering up, and the time in the laboratory or class-room is best spent in taking observations.

PRACTICAL PSYCHOLOGY

PART I

EXPERIMENTAL

CHAPTER I

SENSATION AND PERCEPTION

Visual Acuity

Experiment 1

The standard of visual acuity is defined as the power to distinguish black objects on a white surface which subtend an angle of 5 minutes on the retina. A line of 1·45 mms. at a distance of 1 metre from the eye subtends this angle; and such a line can be distinguished at the distance named by the so-called 'normal' eye. When letters are used, as in Snellen's type sheets, the size of the letters is such as to produce an angle of 5′ vertically and horizontally, the strokes and spaces between the letters subtending an angle of 1′. In the diagram on the next page the lines are 2·9 mms. and therefore subtend an angle of 5′ at a distance of 2 metres, whilst the width of the lines subtends an angle of 1′.

The diagram is placed vertically in front of the subject, who stands with his back to a large northern window with a clear skyline, at a distance of about 4½ metres from the lines. One eye is shaded but not closed, and by means of a slit in a cardboard screen each of the five horizontal series of lines is exposed by the experimenter in a prearranged order. The subject calls out the number of lines, and if he makes any mistake he moves nearer about ½ metre each time until he reaches a critical point at which he makes no mistakes. At each distance, in order to prevent guessing, two blanks are introduced at irregular intervals into the series, and these must be correctly discriminated. The lines are shown in a different order at each distance. When the 5 series and

FIG. 1.

the blanks have been correctly discerned the subject moves nearer to the diagram and the whole process is repeated as he steps backward ½ metre at a time. In this way another critical point is found. The distances are measured by a cord from the diagram to the eye. The mean of the two critical distances is the subject's threshold. The standard distance for these lines is 2 metres, and

$$\text{visual acuity} = \frac{\text{threshold}}{\text{standard}}.$$

Each eye should be tested in turn, with and without glasses. The eye is easily fatiguable, and therefore subject and experimenter should change places after each eye is tested.

A useful topic for investigation may be made out of the following extension of the experiment. The lines are printed in different colours and the threshold for different colours may be determined. A table is drawn up:

Colour	*Threshold* (*Cms.*)	*Percentage of Black*
Black		
Blue		
Red		
Green		
Yellow		

The figures in the third column are found by dividing each threshold by the value of the threshold for black, in good daylight. The usual order is that given in the table; but there are interesting individual variations worthy of careful investigation.

Note on the Limiting Method.—The method used in this experiment is a crude instance of the limiting method, or the method of minimal change. As the subject approaches or recedes from the diagram, the size of the retinal image, which may be called the stimulus, increases or decreases. It is obviously the same whether the diagram is moved or the subject moves. The magnitude of the stimulus which is just discernible, or what comes to the same thing, the distance at which the lines may be separately distinguished, is called the liminal (limen =

threshold) stimulus. The sensation, as it were, is lifted over the *threshold* from sub-consciousness to consciousness. The stimulus must attain a certain magnitude in order to produce a definite sensation. The limiting method is one of the psycho-physical methods, the object of the procedure being such as to ensure that the threshold is determined fairly and, as far as possible, to eliminate random guesses. The stimulus, therefore, is slowly increased or decreased in size. There is an indefinite region of uncertainty between the critical points where the subject sometimes succeeds and sometimes fails, and by the limiting method we attempt to determine as exactly as possible the point within this region where the threshold is just crossed.

Auditory Acuity

Experiment 2

The object of this experiment is to determine the threshold for auditory acuity.

The method used, as in the case of vision, is a simple form of the limiting method. The experimenter prepares four series of 10 figures each and practises repeating them in a 'forced whisper,' saying each number at the end of an expiration. When he can do this readily, he seats the subject at a distance of 20 feet away in a large room with his right ear towards himself. The left ear should be plugged with a rubber stopper, and the mouth of the subject must be closed. A few test figures are now repeated in forced whisper to accustom the subject to the conditions. Before whispering each figure the experimenter makes a signal by a sharp rap so as to engage the attention of the subject. The subject is instructed to write down each number as he hears it, and to make a stroke if he fails. In this way a series of 10 numbers is repeated, then a short rest is taken, and the next 10 is repeated, and so on. When the whole four series is finished the experimenter moves 5 feet towards the subject and repeats the whole four series again. The operation is repeated, at successive distances, until the experimenter is 5 feet from the subject. He then steps backwards 5 feet at a time and repeats the series in the same way.

Both ears are tested in this way; and subject and experimenter change rôles after each ear is tested, for the sake of variety.

Binaural hearing may be measured in the same way, by allowing the subject to face the experimenter, the eyes being closed or shaded.

By sorting out the number of figures correctly heard at each distance, a rough idea of the threshold of auditory acuity may be obtained. That distance at which 80 to 90 per cent. of the figures are correctly recorded may be arbitrarily selected as the threshold. As in the previous experiment, the threshold is determined both inwards and outwards and the mean of the two is taken as the final result.

A similar method may be employed with a stop watch. In this case the experimenter moves forwards or backwards ½ to 1 metre at a time. At each distance the watch is set going, after a prearranged signal, 5 times; but 2 'catches' are introduced at each distance. The subject calls out if he hears the watch. The threshold is the distance at which he makes no blunders. The watch test produces much more variable results and is greatly affected by practice. If time permits the whisper test should be employed in preference to the watch test.

Perception

Experiment 3

The purpose of this experiment is twofold: to find out what difference is made in observation by a preliminary systematic knowledge of what one is about to observe, and also the part played in observation by an adequate terminology.

The material selected consists of suits of armour (see Appendix I.), since these have a definite describable form and each part has a technical name. In these respects the material is comparable in use to the description of an animal in zoology or a plant in botany. The experiment is suitable for class work and may be applied to a form in a school equally well. The pictures may be converted into lantern slides if necessary.

The demonstrator states the object of the experiment as above, and tells the class that they will be shown pictures of armour and that they will be asked afterwards to describe in writing everything they have observed. He states also that sufficient time will be given for observation and that incorrect descriptions will be penalised. The method of marking is also explained to the subjects: 2 marks for each *part* correctly noted, 1 mark for each *position* correctly stated, 1 mark for each *description* correctly noted. The same marks with a negative sign are given for incorrect observations. This scheme of marking should be illustrated by pointing to a chair or table in the room. A *part* would be such things as the seat, the splats, the legs, etc.; a *position* means that the table is turned to the right or is a foot from the chair, etc.; a *description* consists of such things as a round or bevelled top, regular grain, etc.

Before the experiment begins, sheets of paper are prepared by the subjects, divided thus:

SUBJECT : EXPERIMENTER : DATE :

	Details Remembered	*General Observations*
1		
2		
3		
4		
5		
6		
7		
8		
9		

On the left-hand side every detail that has been observed is recorded in brief catalogue form; on the right are included general observations which cannot be conveniently classified under detail. At the bottom of the sheet the following sentence is written and signed by the subject before the sheet is given up. "I have tried, but cannot remember anything else." At the back of the sheet introspective observations are recorded, i.e. feelings, emotions, attitudes, moods, sensations, and so on.

When all the above preliminaries are settled, Picture 1 is shown for precisely $1\frac{1}{2}$ minutes. It is then withdrawn and each subject fills in his observations immediately afterwards from memory. When the statements are signed and introspections recorded, the sheets are interchanged amongst the subjects who mark each other's papers, with the picture in front of them. Picture 2 is then dealt with in exactly the same way.

As some practice is necessary in order to adjust oneself to the experimental conditions the marks obtained for Picture 1, though recorded in notebooks, may be ignored, and the class divided up into equivalent Groups L and N on the basis of the marks obtained on Picture 2 alone. The standard deviation of the whole class is used as unit of measurement all through the experiment.

The lecture on armour (see Appendix I.) is now given to the Group L, the other group being dismissed. All the terms are illustrated by the sheet of parts shown in the Appendix, and the group study the technical terms during the following week until they know them perfectly.

Experiment 4

A week after the above experiment the Groups L and N are recombined and Pictures 3 and 4, are treated as above described. The subjects of each group mark the papers within that group to avoid the difficulty of the technical terms. It will be seen that Pictures 3 and 4 are much more elaborate than 1 and 2, the object being to discover in what manner preperception puts the subject in a better position for ignoring irrelevant and confusing detail. Marks being assigned on the same method as before, the average mark of each subject (measured in terms of the standard deviation) for Pictures 3 and 4 are found. A quantitative estimate of the effects of preperception may now be made by comparing the marks of the trained with the untrained groups.

A qualitative comparison is possible by obtaining written replies to the following questions:

For Group L:

(1) Did the lecture aid you in taking in the picture, and, if so, precisely in what way?

(2) Did the technical terms help you to remember what you had taken in, and to observe more efficiently?

Give your own introspections quite apart from any theory you have on the matter.

(3) Did the ornamentation on the last two pictures interfere with your observation ? If so, how ?

For Group N:

(1) Did lack of technical terms prevent your taking in the pictures during observation ?

(2) Did lack of terms prevent you from remembering what you had observed ?

(3) Did the ornamentation on the last two pictures interfere with your observation ? If so, how ?

These quantitative and qualitative results should enable the subjects to verify or refute the following theory of perception: The only things we perceive are those which we preperceive; and the only things we preperceive are those which we can name (James).

A full discussion of results will be found in the author's *Educational Psychology*, Ch. III.

CHAPTER II

HABIT FORMATION

The Attainment Curve

Experiment 5

The purpose of this experiment is to study the rate of growth of a habit, with reference to attainments.

A demonstrator acts as experimenter and the members of the class as subjects.

Several sheets of continuous texts (see Appendix II.) are used. The experimenter reads the following instructions aloud to the subjects: "You are provided with a number of sheets containing texts in which the words are all run together. There are no divisions between words or paragraphs and no punctuation marks; so that the text has simply the appearance of a continuous series of letters. You are required to make bold vertical lines in pencil between the letters so as to divide them into words. Wherever you think a full stop is necessary make a bold cross on top of the vertical line you have previously drawn, but ignore all other punctuation. When a signal is given by striking the table draw a horizontal line under the last word you have completed so as to take in all the letters of the word. Work as accurately and carefully as possible. Avoid all hurry and make all lines and crosses as neatly and boldly as you can. If you hurry you will penalise yourself heavily by unnecessary loss of marks. No erasures or crossings out are permitted. If you have made a mistake, pass on to the next word without alteration."

If the texts in the Appendix are used a sheet of tracing paper may be employed, tied down with an elastic band or stuck so as not to move. Otherwise the texts may be reproduced by photography.

It is a good plan, at this point, to show the method on the blackboard with short selected sentences not occurring in the texts. The necessity of working carefully, without hurry should be emphasised.

The experimenter, with a stop watch in front of him, gives the signal to start, and the subjects work continuously for 5 minutes. At the end of each minute a signal is made and the word "Horizontal" called out; and at the end of the 5-minute period the experimenter calls "Stop." The sheets are then turned over and an interval of 1 or 2 minutes' rest is given filled up with conversation on irrelevant topics. The same procedure is then followed with all the remaining sheets. At the end of the whole experiment each subject writes an introspective account of his feelings and procedure, paying special attention to his acquirement of facility in the task and making some attempt to explain what factors play a part in increasing facility.

The records are entered thus:

SUBJECT : EXPERIMENTER : DATE:

Intervals	*Marks*	*Introspections*
1 minute		
2 minutes		
3 ,,		
4 ,,		
5 ,,		
6 ,,		
7 ,,		
8 ,,		
9 ,,		
10 ,,		

The worked papers are interchanged amongst the subjects and marked on the following plan:

1 mark for each word correctly indicated.

2 marks for each full stop correctly shown.

Marks are subtracted for the following errors:

1 for an omitted stroke.

1 for a stroke through a letter instead of between letters.

2 for a full stop incorrectly placed or omitted.

1 for a stroke which incorrectly divides the words. (Note that in such a case 3 marks are lost, since 1 is subtracted and 2 are lost for the two words. If this is made clear to the subjects, accuracy is ensured.)

Two curves are now drawn—individual curves in which marks are plotted as ordinates against intervals as abscissæ; a group curve in which the median mark of the whole class for each minute is plotted against the corresponding intervals. If sufficient points are obtained and the group curve is smoothed out the formula of the attainment curve may be obtained.

This curve should be compared with that of the sending curve of Bryan and Harter (see the author's *Educational Psychology*, p. 112) which was obtained by a very similar method to the above experiment.

Experiment 6

In the previous experiment the curve of progress in attainments was mapped out, over equal practice periods of time. The present experiment is to test attainments after equal amounts of practice.

The construction of the following code is explained to the subjects by the experimenter, and a word such as 'acknowledge' is written on the board in code symbols so as to show its use. Any other code will do equally well, and should be used if the subjects know the one here presented.

The subjects are then given 2 minutes in which to memorise the code, after which it is removed and not allowed to be seen again during the experiment. They are told to learn it so as to be able to use it from memory.

Twenty lines of suitable text, such as *Paradise Lost*, are selected and the subjects transcribe the first two lines at their own pace. They are instructed to write only from their memory image of the code and not to copy their own previous writing nor to sketch the code on paper. When all have transcribed two lines a signal is given and their attainment is tested by transcribing as much as possible of the first of the lines of alphabet (Appendix III.) in 45 seconds. After a brief rest the process is repeated with the next two lines of *Paradise Lost* and the second line of letters; and so on till the whole 20 lines

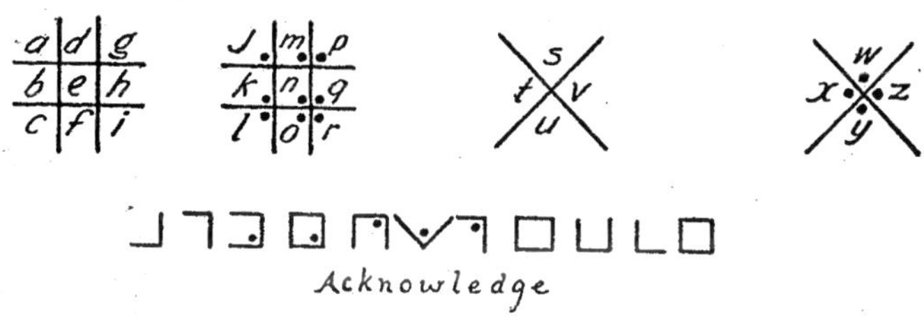

FIG. 2.

and the ten series of alphabets have been transcribed into the code.

Before the subjects transcribe the alphabets the experimenter should insist that the letters must be copied *in the exact order in which they occur,* and that if a person finishes a line of letters before the signal to stop is given he must go back to the beginning and repeat the same line. It is hardly likely that a subject will finish a line at any stage of the practice in 45 seconds, but cases sometimes occur. An alternative method is to find the time the subject takes to transcribe a line of letters.

As soon as the last line of letters has been transcribed a

careful introspective record is taken, and this should be regarded as the essential part of the experiment. The following questions must be answered in some detail: (*a*) How did the subject work from the code during the transcription? (*b*) Did he have a definite mental image? If so what was its nature? (*c*) Whether he was conscious at any stage of improved facility, and what was it due to? (*d*) What happened to the image as practice increased?

The alphabets are marked in the following way:

1 mark for each letter correctly transcribed.

1 mark is deducted for each of the following errors: incorrect symbol, omitted letter, omitted dot, added letter, added dot.

Two curves are drawn, an individual and a group curve. In the former the marks are plotted against the number of the test. For the group curve the average number of marks for the whole group for each line of alphabets is plotted. Records are entered thus:

SUBJECT: EXPERIMENTER: DATE:

Number of Line	*Marks*	*Introspections*
1		
2		
3		
4		
5		
6		

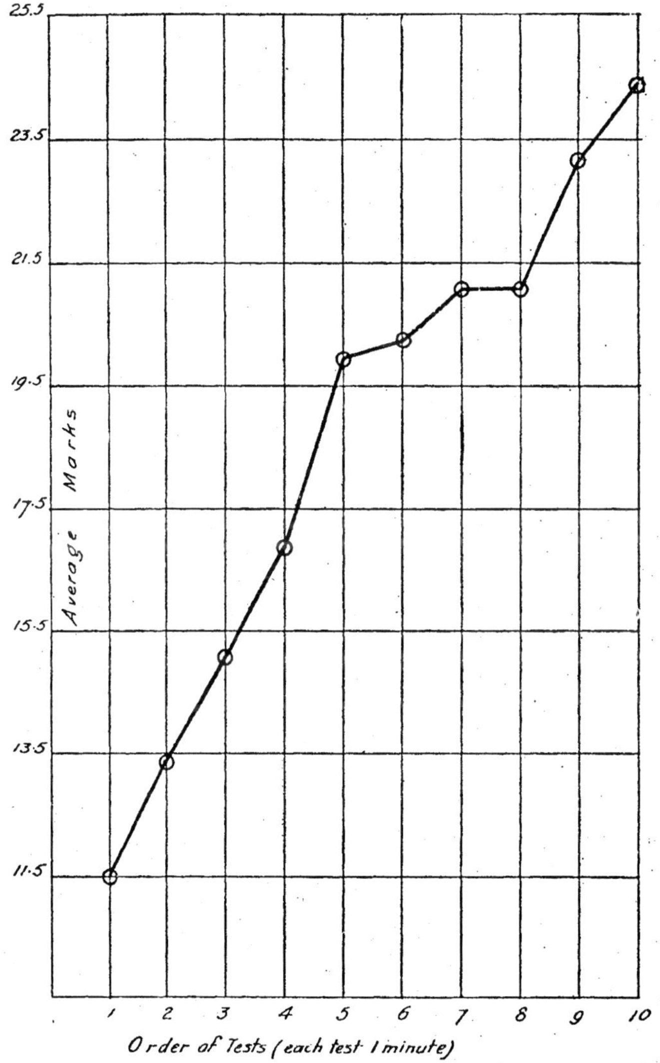

FIG. 3.—CURVE OF ATTAINMENT. CODE WRITING (26 SUBJECTS).

Discussion of Results

Imagery in Learning

The introspective records obtained from this experiment serve to indicate the part played by mental imagery in the process of learning. Great care must be taken in interpreting the results, as the ability to introspect and describe one's own imagery is a difficult art, and untrained subjects are quite untrustworthy with reference to their own imagery. They frequently confuse visual with kinæsthetic images, and both with feelings. One thing, however, is abundantly clear, and may be observed even with untrained subjects, namely that no two persons learn in the same way. Even when the material presented is very precise and definite, as it is here, it is a mistake to assume, that the imagery will be similar in any two persons and still more rash is it to infer what use will be made of the images, supposing they do arise.

It is certain that no subject gets a visual image of the whole code at once. Those who think they do suffer from faulty introspection; just as many people imagine that they see a whole page of print at once, whereas they only 'see' a word or two, as may be easily observed by fixating a word steadily on a printed page and noting how much of the page can be read without moving the eye. Many subjects split up each of the code figures into sections in diverse ways, and a considerable proportion only visualise the individual letters as they use them. In the majority of cases, at the beginning of the experiment, the code figures have to be systematically searched for in alphabetical order until the letter is found; which suggests that the imagery employed is mainly kinæsthetic. Where the person denies this more careful introspection will reveal it. Others fix their attention on the initial letters of each code figure or the middle ones and get the remaining letters from these points of departure; and there is a great variety of other devices employed by different people. Many who assert that they have visual images of the code find, on more careful introspection, that they are really moving along the figures in search for the letters in the same way that a blind man moves his fingers over Braille type, i.e. they make use of oculo-motor or manu-motor images or sensations. Some subjects assert that they are guided by an 'inward voice.' It is evident that little importance can be attached to the widely spread belief that images are the immediate 'residua' of sensational experiences. What particular imagery (if any) a person will employ in learning depends on his mental make-up and not primarily on the sensory material presented.

As the experiment progresses certain letters come to be written without reference to the code at all. This is shown by the fact that the person may sometimes write the symbol and think it is incorrect, whereas a search through the mental code shows that the letter is correctly transcribed. Gradually, certain combinations of letters or frequently occurring words or phrases become automatic. Sooner or later, in the case of every person, the image entirely disappears and the printed letters suggest the code symbols without reference to the image; which is precisely what happens in ordinary writing. At this stage the code symbols come 'without thinking,' the image dies away and is only resuscitated when for any reason some difficulty arises, or as it is said the person 'is stuck.' In the free flow of thinking or acting images play no part.

The Time Curve

Experiment 7

The purpose of this experiment is to study the rate of growth of a habit, with reference to time.

The accompanying diagram shows the apparatus to be used. The essential part of the arrangement is a metal plate (A) pierced in the centre and in the form of a hexagon; each hole being numbered. Below the plate is put a sheet of paper (B) resting on a felt pad, and the whole is placed in front of a plane mirror (C). The dotted part of the diagram (D) is a cardboard screen, bent forwards in the top half so as to hide the plate and the subject's hand during the experiment. By this means the subject can only see the pierced plate and his hand by looking over the screen into the mirror, and should not be allowed to look round the screen at his hand during the whole course of the experiment. The task of the subject is to pierce the holes in a definite prescribed order, guiding his movements by what he sees in the mirror. In other words, he tries to make his mirror-hand subservient to his will.

It is the task of the experimenter strictly to carry out the following instructions, and never to allow the subject

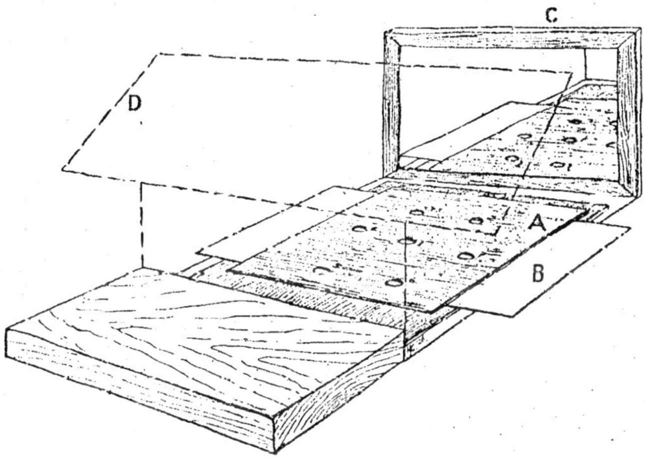

FIG. 4.

A. Metal plate
B. Sheet of paper
C. Mirror
D. Cardboard screen

to arrange the apparatus. The subject takes a knitting needle and the experimenter guides his hand to the central hole, placing the needle lightly on the paper, where it is held until a signal is given. The subject is told that he must pierce the middle hole when the signal is made, and then *lift* the needle to the rest of the numbered holes, in a prescribed order, and pierce the paper each time.

No variation is to be allowed and the serial order of pricking the paper must be the same throughout the whole experiment. If the subject appears to want to try a different order he should be cautioned immediately. It is essential that the needle be *lifted* from hole to hole, and the subject should not be allowed to slide it along the plate. Those who work rapidly tend to slide unless carefully watched by the experimenter. Further, the subject must not be allowed to place the needle in the middle hole by himself, but the hand must be guided there by the experimenter at the beginning of each experiment.

When one series of 7 holes has been pierced, a new sheet of paper is inserted. As each sheet is withdrawn it is numbered, and the time to perform the task is recorded on it. The time is taken by a stop watch, in fifths of a second, from the moment the signal is given until the subject has pierced the last hole. The whole operation is repeated fifty times, but the subject is not informed of his results until the end of the experiment.

After the 20th, 40th, and 50th readings the subject dictates his introspections to the experimenter, who records them literally. Such introspections are chiefly devoted to a consideration (1) of the difficulties experienced in performing the process, (2) and how these were overcome.

When the task becomes appreciably easier some attempt should be made to state precisely by introspection how the facility is *felt*. Certain holes are much more difficult to arrive at than others, and the introspections should be stated more fully with regard to these. All muscular, sensational, and imaginal experiences should be stated. Unless the subject gives the information spontaneously, he should be asked, after the final reading, what particular procedure be adopted in finding the various holes, whether by calculation, trial and error, or in other ways.

The readings are entered thus:

SUBJECT : EXPERIMENTER : DATE :

Attempts	*Time Taken*	*Introspections*
1		
2		
3		
4		
5		
6		
7		
8		
9		

Two curves are now constructed, an individual curve and a group curve, the times in each case being plotted as ordinates against the number of the attempts as abscissæ.

The readings recorded in the table above give the data for the individual curve, which is plotted without smoothing; whilst the group curve is constructed in the following manner: The times for each individual in the class for each attempt are grouped together, and the *median* time of the whole group for each attempt is found. The ordinates are the median times, and the abscissæ, as before, are spaced at equal intervals. A smooth curve which best fits the reading may now be drawn through the ordinates. Such a method of double smoothing has the advantage of eliminating any marked variations due to peculiar individuals or to accidental causes, since the median, unlike the mean, is not affected by unduly large or small readings. Each student should enter his own and the group curves in his notebook, and these may be superimposed on each other for purposes of comparison.

Interpretation of Results.—The group smoothed curve shows the rate at which the habit is developing, and the law of development, based on a large number of groups, may be summarised in the following form:

$$t=\frac{K}{(n+p)^c}+T.$$

In this expression t represents the time necessary to perform the complete operation of piercing all the holes; n is the number of the attempt; c is a small number greater than unity and probably less than 2; and K, p, and T are constants. Every person has pierced holes before the experiment and has performed such operations as dressing whilst looking in a mirror, and the constant p is a measure of the extent that such operations have helped the new task. K is a measure of the difficulty of the task and the subject's capacity in its performance.

The larger n becomes, the smaller the time necessary to perform the operation, until the first expression on the right-hand side of the equation becomes negligible. When this stage is reached the person is said to be on the plateau; and T measures the time required for the operation when the subject has reached his limiting capacity. When the group curve is constructed the formula should be tested. (For a discussion of this curve see the author's *Educational Psychology*, Ch. V., p. 135.)

Whilst the group curve shows the general law of growth the individual curves, though following the same general course, indicate great variations from subject to subject. The introspections will reveal the fact that there are great individual differences in the mode of learning; there are, in fact, almost as many methods of learning as there are subjects who perform the experiment. It is highly probable that no subject learns simply by groping, i.e. by trial and error. All of them make some definite method or plan. The more cautious calculate in advance which way the hand ought to move, others see the hand moving the wrong way and then correct it, others just dash at the holes and correct errors as they come, and so on indefinitely. It may sometimes happen that a subject is quite incapable of moving to a particular hole for some time, no matter how hard he tries—he seems to be paralysed. Such cases would make a useful topic for research. Sooner or later the subject finds that no matter what his method may be he will do better to ignore it and trust his mirror-hand to carry out the movements. On the other hand, several subjects find that the action becomes mechanical without their being aware of it; that the facility grows unconsciously. When this stage is reached, it is an indication that the subject is near the plateau and will not improve very much.

A very instructive phenomenon from the point of view of the development of spatial perception and one which is well worthy of extended investigation may be frequently observed. The subject comes to regard the mirror-hand as a new organ. He does not, after much practice, think of his real hand at all, but only of the seen hand. When he gets tired or cramped these sensations are referred to the hand seen in the mirror, and the muscular movements he makes are also referred to the same space. This appears to show that the localisation of our sensations of touch and movement partly depends on our sense of sight, so that we tend to localise touches and strains, where we see them. And the same thing may be detected with regard to pain in the fingers. In brief, all these sensations are projected into the mirror.

Experiment 8

This experiment is a necessary preliminary to that which follows; its main purpose being to secure practice in a particular kind of habit formation.

Each member of the class constructs series of nonsense syllables, each consisting of two different consonants with an intervening vowel. The following rules must be strictly observed in making such series, in order to eliminate meaning as far as may be. If this is done a series of meaningless monosyllables is provided with which to habituate the vocal muscles: (1) No syllable must directly suggest a sensible word; (2) the initial consonants must not be the same unless separated by two or more syllables; (3) final consonants and vowels should also obey the preceding rule; (4) the initial consonant of one syllable must not be the same as the final consonant of the preceding syllable; (5) two consecutive syllables must not form a sensible word; (6) no two letters of one syllable should recur in any other.

Following these rules, each subject constructs three separate series of 9, 12, and 15 syllables respectively. The syllables are printed under each other in block capitals on separate cards and are covered by a larger card, which has a slit just wide enough to allow one syllable to be seen at a time. In learning any series the writing is covered by the larger card, the slit of which is drawn past the syllables so that they appear at a uniform rate. It is necessary to use a metronome, making 65 to 70 beats to the minute, and at each beat a syllable is exposed by the experimenter. By interchanging the series amongst the members of the class, each person learns three sets of each length, and is heard as soon as he knows them. The syllables are exposed by the experimenter at the metronome rate, and he makes a mark after each repetition. As soon as the subject thinks he knows a series he repeats them without looking, and, if he fails, he continues the series, counting his failure as one repetition. When a subject has learnt 3 series of syllables the average number of repetitions required is recorded. At this stage subject and experimenter change rôles in order to avoid fatigue. The process is then repeated with the series of 12, and finally with that of 15. The results are recorded thus:

Length of series	9	12	15
Average number of repetitions			

By averaging the number for the whole class some idea may be obtained of the increase of the number of repetitions with the length of the series. Ebbinghaus, the inventor of the method, obtained the following figures:

Length of series	12	16	24	36
Number of repetitions ..	16·6	30	44	55

Experiment 9

The purpose of this experiment is to verify the logarithmic law expressing the rate of decay of a habit.

This experiment should only be attempted by those who have done the previous experiment, owing to the necessity of preliminary practice in securing a proper adjustment to the experimental conditions. All the precautions suggested in the earlier experiment should be strictly adhered to in this. It is especially important to learn the syllables at a fixed metronome rate of 65 to 70 beats per minute.

Different sets of 15 nonsense syllables are prepared. Two such sets are learnt by each subject and the average number of repetitions necessary to repeat them by heart is recorded. In order to avoid fatigue each person acts as subject and experimenter in turn, interchanging after each set has been learnt.

On the basis of the average marks obtained, the class is divided into 3 groups—(*a*), (*b*), and (*c*)—of equal ability in this sort of learning.

All the subjects then proceed to learn the same new set of 15 syllables. For this set each person must do his own recording, which is accomplished by making a stroke on paper after each repetition, and trying, when he thinks he knows them, to say the syllables before they appear through the slit in the card. In addition, he must record by his watch the time of the final repetition, i.e. the time when the learning is complete.

Group (*a*) find out the number of repetitions required to relearn the final set 15 minutes after the completion of learning. Group (*b*) do the same thing 30 minutes after learning, and group (*c*) at an interval of 45 or 60 minutes. This procedure yields a measure of the amount retained and the amount forgotten by initially equivalent groups for three different intervals of time.

The results are entered thus:

Number of Repetitions Required to Learn	*Number of Repetitions Required to Re-learn after . . . Minutes*	*Amount Retained*	*Amount Forgotten*	$m = \frac{\text{Amount Retained}}{\text{Amount Forgotten}}$
24	8	16	8	2·00
24	9	15	9	1·67

Expressed in symbols Ebbinghaus' law of forgetting states

$$m = \frac{\text{K}}{(\log t)^c}$$

K and c are constants and t is the time in minutes since the end of the learning. When the average value of m for each of the three groups has been calculated, in the above fashion, we have 3 equations which, if taken in pairs, yield 3 values of c. If these are approximately the same the law may be regarded as verified. By the method of this experiment, which differs from that of Ebbinghaus, the value of c is approximately 3.

Piéron has a different formula which may be tested by a similar method.

$$\text{M} = \frac{\text{K}(\log t)^a}{t^b}$$

M in this formula is the percentage economy in the number of repetitions, and t is measured in days. He suggested a simpler formula which may also be tested, namely, where n is greater than unity

$$\text{M} = \frac{\text{K}}{\sqrt[n]{t}}.$$

CHAPTER III

MENTAL IMAGERY

Imagery

Experiment 10

This experiment serves to investigate the chief varieties of the subjects' voluntarily evoked imagery. Use is made of an abbreviated and slightly modified form of Dr. Bett's questionnaire (see *Distribution and Functions of Imagery*, Columbia University Press). The student should carefully note that the ability to evoke images belonging to any of the categories named does not imply that such images are ordinarily used in thinking.

The instructions and the questionnaire are given on p. 33.

SUBJECT : EXPERIMENTER : DATE :

	Visual	*Auditory*	*Kinæsthetic*
Question 1			
,, 2			
,, 3			
,, 4			
,, 5			
,, 6			
,, 7			
,, 8			
,, 9			
,, 10			
,, 11			
,, 12			
,, 13			
,, 14			
,, 15			
,, 16			

The directions should be carefully read and the Key consulted for each question. A sheet is prepared in the form given on p. 31.

The various columns are filled up with the appropriate figures or grades by the help of the Key. From the figures so obtained another table is made:

Grades	*Number of Visual Images*	*Score*	*Number of Auditory Images*	*Score*	*Number of Kinæsthetic Images*	*Score*
Grade 1						
,, 2						
,, 3						
,, 4						
,, 5						
,, 6						
,, 7						
	Total		Total		Total	

In order to get the score multiply the number of images in each grade by the number of the grade. The total scores thus obtained indicate the relative ability in each sort of imagery, care being taken to observe that the lower the score the better the imagery.

If the results for the whole class are grouped together in a table similar to the above, histograms for the three main kinds of imagery may be constructed; and it will usually be found that the distribution is approximately of the same form for each (see p. 37).

Questionnaire upon Mental Imagery

Directions

The 7 grades or degrees of clearness and vividness printed in the Key below will give you a standard by which to determine your answers to the questions on the tests. Read and re-read this page until you fully understand what each grade or degree means. Keep this page before you as you answer the questions, and refer to it constantly in deciding what your answers shall be. Please answer *all* the questions. Simply write the *number* (3, 5, 2, etc.) which corresponds to the degree of clearness and vividness upon which you decide for your image. Do not hurry in answering the questions, and answer each strictly upon its own merits, that is, regardless of how you have answered any other one.

Key for Answering Questions

Grades

With respect to the mental picture suggested in each of the questions of the test, is the image which comes before your mind—

1. Perfectly clear and as vivid as the actual experience, *or*
2. Very clear and comparable in vividness to the actual experience, *or*
3. Moderately clear and vivid, *or*
4. Not clear or vivid, but recognisable, *or*
5. Vague and dim, *or*
6. So vague and dim as to be hardly discernible, *or*
7. No object present at all, you only *knowing in some other way* that you are thinking of the object.

Visual Imagery

I. Think of your breakfast table as you sat down to it this morning, considering carefully the picture that rises before your mind's eye, and classify the images suggested by each of the following questions as indicated by the degrees of clearness and vividness specified in the Key:

A. As to outline, or shape and size.

1. The table as a whole seen at one glance.
2. The different dishes, e.g., cups, plates, etc.

B. As to colours.

3. Colour of the table cloth and napkins.
4. Colours of the dishes.

II. Think of somebody whom you frequently see, considering carefully the picture that rises before your mind's eye, and classify the images suggested by each of the following questions as indicated by the degrees of clearness and vividness specified in the Key:

A. As to form, feature, etc.

5. The exact contour of face, head, shoulders, and body.
6. Characteristic poses of head, attitudes of body, etc.

B. As to colours.

7. The exact complexion, both as to colour and clearness of skin.
8. The precise shade of colour of the hair.

III. Recall some familiar landscape which you have recently seen, considering carefully the pictures which rise before your mind's eye; and classify the image suggested by each of the following questions as indicated by the degrees of clearness and vividness specified in the Key:

A. As to distance, size, etc.

9. The scene as a whole, actual size, distance, etc.
10. The difference in sharpness of details between near or distant objects.

B. As to light and colour.

11. The different shades and tints in the sky or clouds.
12. The different shades of green in grass, of grey in clouds.

IV. Read carefully the following:

" Him the Almighty Power
Hurled headlong flaming from the ethereal sky,
With hideous ruin and combustion, down
To bottomless perdition, there to dwell
In adamantine chains and penal fire."

Now classify the images which rose before the mind's eye as directed by the degrees of clearness and vividness specified in the Key:

A. As to form and movement.

13. The falling of Satan.
14. His bound position in perdition.

B. As to colours and light.

15. The degree of brightness in the sky.
16. The colours of the flames in perdition.

Auditory Imagery

I. Think of a friend saying, " I will call for you as soon as I am ready." Consider carefully the image of his voice which comes to your mind's ear, and classify the images suggested by each of the following questions as indicated by the degrees of clearness and vividness as specified in the Key.

1. The exact quality as different from all other voices.
2. The articulation and pronunciation used.
3. The amount of force or loudness.
4. The precise pitch.

II. Recall some perfectly familiar tune; and classify the images you experience by aid of the Key:

5. As played on a piano.
6. As sung by a friend's voice.

III. Think of each of the following sounds, consider the sound images carefully, and classify them by means of the Key:

7. The beat of rain against the window.
8. The whistle of a locomotive.
9. The clink of glasses.
10. The slam of a door.
11. The mewing of a cat.
12. The clapping of hands in applause.
13. The rattling of a newspaper.
14. The droning of an aeroplane.
15. The sound of a clock striking.
16. The buzzing of flies.

Kinæsthetic Imagery

Think of performing each of the following acts, considering carefully the *image* (do not confuse this with the incipient movement of the muscles concerned) which you receive in your mind's 'arms,' 'legs,' 'lips,' etc., and classify the images as indicated by the Key. *Avoid in each case confusing the motor image with the visual image of seeing yourself doing these things.*

1. Running upstairs.
2. Drawing a circle on paper.
3. Writing your name.
4. Lifting a heavy weight.
5. Reaching up to a high shelf.
6. Nodding your head in assent.
7. Rising out of a low chair.
8. Moving your eyes sideways.
9. Waving your hand to a friend.
10. Counting to 10 orally as fast as you can.
11. Throwing a ball.
12. Kicking something out of your way.
13. Stooping down to tie your shoe.
14. Putting your hand round your neck.
15. Passing a heavy dish at the table.
16. Tilting the head back to look at some object high above you.

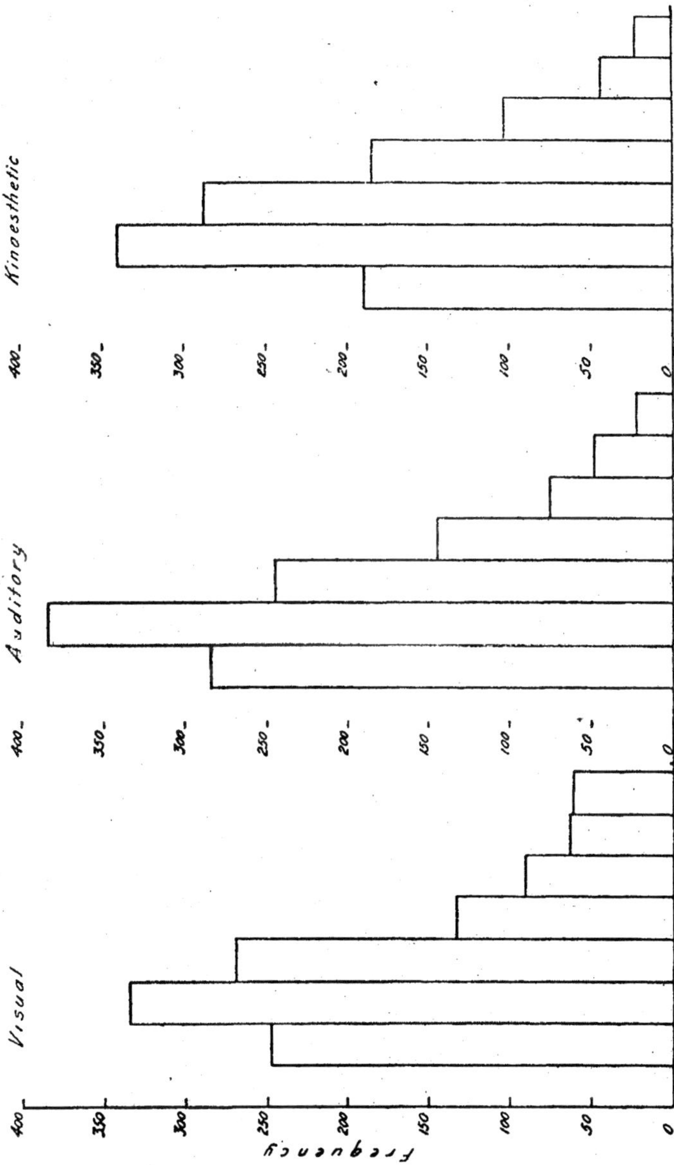

FIG. 5.—SHOWING DISTRIBUTION OF MENTAL IMAGERY OF 75 SUBJECTS ACCORDING TO DEGREE OF VIVIDNESS AND CLEARNESS.

Experiment 11

The following experiment is intended to be an exercise in the investigation of the imagery employed in solving geometrical problems or those of a like kind. The tests are given below and others of a similar nature may easily be constructed.

One minute is allowed for each question. The subject places his hand on the desk so as to prevent him from drawing diagrams on the paper or tracing them in the air. A signal is given to start and stop each question, and the person must not go back or forward to other questions.

One mark is given for each correct answer; except questions 6 and 7 where ½ mark is given for each subdivision, i.e. 1½ for each question, and question 9 where 1 mark is given for each reply, i.e. 2. The maximum mark is, therefore, 12.

Tests of Imagery

You must make no sketches either on paper or in the air; nor write anything, except the answer. Keep your hand resting on the table.

1. My house faces the street. If a boy passes my house in the morning walking towards the rising sun, with my house on his right, in which direction does my house face ?

2. I walk direct East for 500 yards, then straight South for another 500 yards. In what direction must I now walk to reach my starting point by the shortest route ?

3. A 3-inch cube painted red is sawn into 1-inch cubes. How many of the little cubes have paint on three faces ?

4. How many have paint on two faces only ?

5. An equilateral triangle has two straight lines drawn from an angle to the opposite side dividing that side into three equal

parts. Suppose now that straight lines are drawn from each of the other two angles to the opposite sides so as to bisect each of the remaining sides. Into how many parts is the original triangle divided?

6. A clock has letters of the alphabet in order instead of figures, starting from the letter M where the figure 1 should be: To what letters does the long hand point at twenty past 12, five minutes to 4, twenty-five minutes to 5?

7. Between what letters is the small hand at 7.35, 9.20, and 11.15?

8. If a boy stands on his head with his face to the South and his arms outstretched, in what direction will his right hand point?

9. Think of the front of the Senate House. Count the number of the pillars you can see and also the number of windows. (Any other large well-known building may be substituted for Senate House, where necessary.)

10. I keep pointing my arm straight forward; first I wheel through an angle of 60 degrees, then back again through an angle of 90 degrees. Next I turn round. What is the size of the angle between the original and final position of my arm?

Discussion of Results.—A good exercise is to find the correlation between the marks in this and the various categories of the preceding experiment. Valuable data would be obtained by trying these tests on school children of different ages and determining the norms for each age. It would be interesting to try to discover whether there is any correlation between excellence in the test and ability in geometry. The test has been tried on twenty-one University graduates with the following results, the marks given for each question being the total for the whole group.

Question	1	2	3	4	5	6	7	8	9	10	Average
Marks	19	19	14	8	2	24½	17½	13	9	10	6½

For the twenty-one graduates the scores obtained in the previous experiment on voluntarily evoked images and those derived from this test were correlated. There was no significant correlation between the scores in the two tests. The highest coefficient was that between the auditory imagery and the test scores where the figure obtained was exactly equal to the probable error. It appears that the imagery employed by these subjects is purely verbal; but further investigation would be necessary to establish this. Another explanation of this curious result may be that no discoverable imagery is used, for in the code experiment (No. 6) on habit we saw that imagery tends to disappear with use. And the images which would originally be used in this test have been employed for many years in school work of a similar kind, so that they have long since had time to subside. There is, in other words, a subconscious background containing no definable images which the subject can discriminate, just as the writing on a palimpsest is no longer decipherable except by special artifices.

Experiment 12

The object of this experiment is to investigate the kind of imagery the subject uses in learning a diagram. It is often assumed, purely on *a priori* grounds, that when a person tries to learn what is visually presented he uses visual imagery, and similarly with the other varieties of presented material. This experiment serves to throw light on the problem.

The subject is required to learn to reproduce the given diagram. The diagram A is exposed to the subject for exactly 5 seconds. A convenient method is to draw it on a card placed between the pages of a book. Immediately afterwards he makes an attempt at reproduction. The experimenter takes the reproduction and does not allow the subject to see it again. After a brief interval of a few seconds the diagram is again exposed, and another attempt at reproduction is made. This process is repeated until the figure is correctly reproduced three times in succession. Correct reproduction is to be interpreted thus: The lines should be approximately of the same proportional length as the diagram, and cut each other at approximately the correct distances. The angles should be approximately correct, i.e. right, acute, or obtuse as the case may be. These approximations should be *interpreted liberally* and not in a pedantic spirit. In estimating the number of exposures required by any given subject the last two of the three correct reproductions should be omitted.

After correct reproduction there should be a careful introspective exploration of the method by which the subject learnt the diagram. He must state his procedure and method precisely. Vague statements such as "I memorised the lines," "I saw the figure in my mind's eye," etc., should be rejected. He should be closely questioned to discover whether he used visual, kinæsthetic, oculo-motor, manumotor, voci-motor imagery, etc., especially the last. If he says he used any particular variety of imagery he must state definitely where it was located and be pressed to describe its precise nature. During the introspective period many subjects frequently

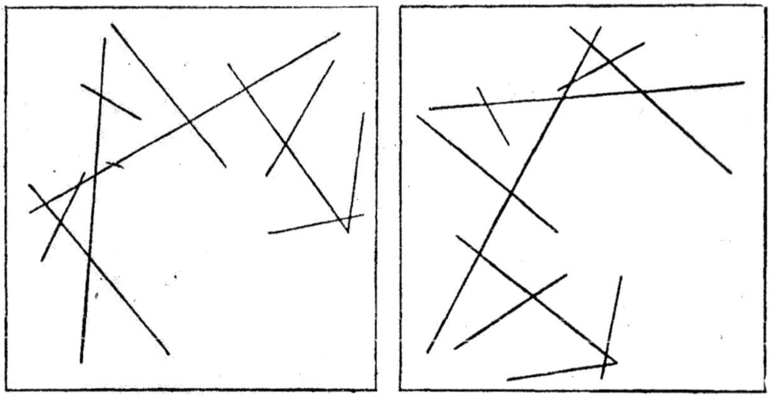

A B

FIG. 6.

change their ground, and their replies are to be recorded verbatim.

Subject and experimenter now change places, and the experiment is repeated with the second diagram, B.

It is a useful exercise to get the same subjects to learn a set of 15 nonsense syllables and to find out whether there is any correlation between the two abilities involved in learning the syllables and the lines. If there is, it suggests strongly that the main factor involved in learning the diagrams is voci-motor imagery. A group of 16 subjects were tested in this way and the correlation coefficient (foot-rule method) was $\cdot 53 \pm \cdot 11$.

Another instructive exercise is to determine the correlation between the rate of forgetting the line diagram and set of nonsense syllables. Fifteen subjects learnt the diagram and a set of 15 syllables on the same day. Forty-nine days later they relearnt both, and the number of repetitions required for learning and relearning was noted. The percentage economy in relearning was then calculated for the separate tasks; and it was found that the correlation between the percentage of repetitions saved on the later day was ·49. This suggests that Piéron's view is correct, namely that the rate of forgetting for both tasks follows the same law.

Discussion of Results.—The average number of exposures to ensure correct reproduction, for adults, is about 13; but the range is very great, from 26 or more to 6 or less. There appears to be no correlation between the ability to evoke any definite sort of imagery and success in this experiment. The number of factors involved, even in such simple learning as this, is considerable, and it is a very difficult task to disentangle them for any particular person. Introspective evidence, unless given by one who has had prolonged experience of introspection work, is almost worthless, and must in every case be carefully checked and probed. Perhaps the most important aid in recalling the diagram is that given by some method of intellectual interpretation of the chaotic appearance, and such interpretation, though frequently verbal, for the most part takes place in rapid judgments of a subconscious kind, in which words hardly play a part. Kinæsthetic imagery (or sensation ?) also plays a predominant part and is of different kinds, oculo-motor, manu-motor, etc.; but this sort of imagery is sketchy and frequently symbolic, suggesting rather than reproducing the diagram. Frequently, too (but this is more difficult to detect), vague feelings arise of a purely affective nature which give the erroneous impression of imagery since they serve to reinstate the feel of the original experience. It often happens, too, that the subject has no recognisable image of any kind and declares roundly that he cannot reproduce the figure (especially after the lapse of some time), yet if pressed to do so his hand produces what he is surprised to recognise as the original diagram. We should be wary of attempting to state *a priori* what the method of learning is for any person and the use made of particular mental imagery in memory.

Experiment 13

This experiment is designed so as to study the process of perceptual learning of skilled movements.

It should be borne in mind that, as far as human beings are concerned, the separation of perceptual from imaginal and ideational processes is an unrealisable ideal. The experimental conditions have been so arranged as to bring into prominence the perceptual part of the learning process and to reduce, as far as may be, the ideational portion. Here, if anywhere, we get an instance

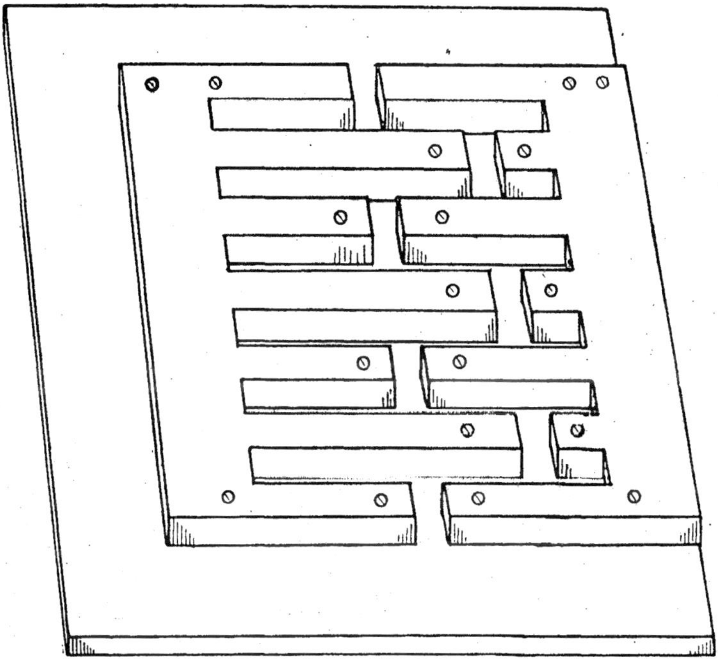

FIG. 7.

of what is called learning by 'trial and error.' The process ought, however, to be called learning by 'trial and success,' for in so far as the subject makes 'errors' his attempts are baulked and only the 'successes' contribute to the learning process.

The maze, here shown in perspective, is constructed of layers of three-ply wood screwed to a base, and its outside dimensions are 12 cms. by 11 cms. The width of the partitions and the grooves are each ·8 cms.; and the depth of the grooves ·7 cms. The base is clamped to a table so that it is firmly fixed and does not slide.

A wooden pointer is used to thread the maze and is thinned at the end so that there is plenty of room on both sides of the pointer and the vertical partitions of the maze. The subject is blindfolded and holds the pointer lightly pressed on the base of the maze, keeping it vertical all the time. Only the pointer should be touched and the hand must not rest on the maze. The following instructions are read by the experimenter: "I shall place a pointer in your hand a short distance in front of the opening of the maze. If you go straight forward you will get into it. Your task is to find the shortest way through the maze without touching the sides. You must not lift the pointer out of the groove, and you must avoid sliding along the sides of the maze. Your task is to learn how to get out of the maze as soon as possible."

The problem is considered to be learnt when the subject has made *three* runs in succession without an error. An error means (1) any attempt at getting through where there is no gap, (2) passing a gap and returning to it, (3) sliding the pointer along the sides of the maze. Number 3 should not be interpreted too pedantically, as quick workers find it difficult to avoid touching the sides occasionally, when near the gaps.

The times of threading the maze are recorded by means of a stop watch, which is started as soon as the subject enters the maze. The subject's hand is guided to the definite mark about half an inch in front of the opening and he moves forward at a prearranged signal. After each trial the subject is engaged in general conversation for a few seconds; and then he makes another attempt, and so on until he has made three successful attempts in succession. In comparing the number of attempts for different subjects the last two readings are ignored. The records are entered thus:

SUBJECT: EXPERIMENTER: DATE:

Attempts	*Times*	*Introspections*
1		
2		
3		
4		
5		
6		
7		

Immediately after learning the subject should be required to draw the maze, before he is allowed to see it.

Finally he dictates his introspections to the experimenter, stating how he learnt the task and more especially what imagery he used: visual, kinæsthetic, verbal, etc.

A time curve may be constructed in which times are plotted against attempts, and this should be compared with the time curve obtained in Experiment 7 on habit formation. If desirable a smoothed group curve can be made, exactly as in this last named experiment, and its form determined. A useful exercise in correlation is obtained by comparing the number of attempts to learn the maze with the number necessary to learn the line diagram.

Discussion of Results.—The following table will be useful in comparing results. The subjects were sixteen graduate students, and the number of attempts is calculated so as to include only the first successful effort. The average time for each subject for the three successful attempts is also given in seconds.

Subjects:	A	B	C	D	E	F	G	H	J	K	L	M	N	O	P	Q	Mean
Attempts:	43	43	34	30	28	24	22	22	22	21	21	20	16	14	13	10	24
Times:	15·7	6·5	6·2	4·6	2·7	12·2	3·4	4·3	2·1	7·1	2·5	5·1	4·7	11·9	8·3	10·6	6·7

There is a suggestion here of a very slight negative correlation between the number of attempts for learning and the time necessary to perform the operation, when the task is known.

It is instructive to note that many subjects learn the problem by establishing a regular rhythmical swing, owing no doubt to the fact that the maze is of a regular form. About half the persons make use of such kinæsthetic rhythmical images in learning the figure, describing their experiences as a 'felt wave motion. A number of subjects make use of verbal images, as 'must go straight, then to the right,' etc. Such verbal imagery is apt to be very much abbreviated, a syllable or a phrase symbolising a whole sentence. Owing to its sketchiness and also the fact that it is difficult to decide whether the words are seen or heard or felt, this sort of imagery escapes careless introspection. In some cases there is no imagery, but the words are actually uttered, in a sketchy form. Other persons make use of visual images, sometimes declaring that they see the line to be followed, clearly marked, standing out against a darker background. In several cases one sort of imagery is used at the beginning and then abandoned later on, not deliberately, but unconsciously; and many subjects use a combination of different kinds of imagery.

The most important thing to note is that the learning process depends largely on the mental make-up of the learner and is not necessarily determined by the nature of the material presented or the mode of using it.

Experiment 14

The purpose of the present experiment is to ascertain the conditions which arouse mental images in directed thought. The twelve statements enumerated below are used; four involve mathematical concepts, four historical, four grammatical, etc. The propositions are read aloud by the experimenter slowly and deliberately, and in such an order that two of a like kind do not follow each other; so that variety and interest may be maintained.

The subjects are instructed to record on a sheet of paper, after the statement is read, whether they realised its meaning, and as soon as the meaning is grasped the process of thought which led to its realisation. In particular they are to state whether the process of thought involved mental images or not. The fact of agreement or disagreement with the propositions is to be stated also, but the important thing is the realisation of the significance of the proposition and the imagery, if any, aroused. In cases where images do arise, the subjects are instructed to state whether the realisation of meaning preceded or succeeded the occurrence of the mental image.

The propositions to be read are:

I*a*. The whole is greater than the part.

I*b*. The whole is equal to the sum of the parts.

I*c*. If equals are added to equals the wholes are equal.

I*d*. If unequals are added to unequals the wholes are unequal.

II*a*. Whilst Britain was prospering under Roman rule the Roman Empire itself was beginning to show signs of decay.

II*b*. Every historical event has a political cause.

II*c*. The whole organisation of society was once based upon the system known as feudalism.

II*d*. Mechanical inventions have had important effects upon the social life of England.

III*a*. All verbs that make a statement must be accompanied by some noun.

IIIb. Grammar is useless because we speak well without a knowledge of it.

IIIc. You should never use a preposition to end a sentence with.

IIId. Laughing to teach the truth
What hinders? As some teachers give to boys
Junkets and knacks, that they may learn apace.

Interpretation of Results.—By classifying the various introspective records relating to the different classes of propositions this experiment will help to show the part played by mental imagery in thought proper as opposed to reverie or day-dreaming. In the latter case images come and go, and we can no more explain the origin of the particular images that arise than we can account for the things we see when we open our eyes. Where, however, there is a definite end in view, a specific problem to be solved, an answer may be possible. For this purpose it is necessary to distinguish between relevant and adventitious images. In a particular train of thought there may be a number of images present which neither aid nor hinder its development—adventitious images.

The following have been shown by the author of this book to be the conditions which arouse relevant images, that is, those which in some way aid the thought process. Any delay or conflict in consciousness is such a condition. Thus, conflict or disagreement with a suggested statement, any attempt to overcome the difficulty of understanding a proposition, suspension of judgment, doubt, all produce images in abundance. The contrary set of conditions are unfavourable to the production of images, that is, thorough or immediate understanding, an easily grasped conception, ready assent to a proposition, straightforward or unimpeded reasoning, etc.

Thus, whatever promotes the easy or unimpeded flow of thought is unfavourable to the production of mental imagery, and *vice versa.*

For a full discussion of the results of this experiment see "The Conditions which Arouse Mental Images in Thought," by C. Fox, *Brit. Journ. of Psychology*, vol. vi., p. 420 ff.

CHAPTER IV

MEMORY

Association Times

Experiment 15

The purpose of this experiment is to study word-associations, and incidentally to get some idea of a method for detecting 'complexes.'

Jung's list of association words is used and a stop watch is required.

The class having been divided up into experimenters and subjects, the experimenter gives the subject the following instruction, precisely in the words here stated: "Answer as quickly as you can, with the first word that comes into your mind." The instruction is repeated and emphasised, but no explanation of it is given; as failure to carry out the instruction is an important part of the experiment. In order to habituate the subject and the experimenter to the procedure, three test words are given as a trial, namely *chapel, talk, good*. The times of these are taken, but not recorded. It is important to adhere strictly to the rule that during the course of the experiment the experimenter should never coach the subject nor correct him, nor give him any information about his times or responses. If the subject asks any questions the experimenter merely replies by repeating the above instruction, and says nothing else. Both the times and the responses are recorded out of sight of the subject. The experimenter's task is simply to record and never to comment.

Prior to the experiment sheets are prepared in the following form, the numbers in the first column referring to the stimulus words, which need not be written on the sheets, but may be read from page 56.

SUBJECT : EXPERIMENTER : DATE :

Stimulus Word	*Reaction Word*	*Reaction Time*	*Reproduction*	*Remarks*
1				
2				
3				
4				
5				
6				
7				

When the above preliminaries are arranged and the 3 test words have been given, the experimenter calls out each stimulus word in order and at the same moment starts the stop watch. The reaction-word is then recorded and the reaction time. A failure to react with a word after 1 minute is recorded as a *fault*. When the complete list of 100 words has been given, an interval of a couple of minutes is allowed to elapse during which the subject is engaged in irrelevant discourse. After this the subject is again given the stimulus words, in order, and is asked to reproduce his former reaction-words. Sufficient time is given and the watch is not used. If he gives any other than his original word it is written in the 4th column or if he fails to give any reply, this is recorded as a *failure*, and the experimenter passes to the next word. In the 5th column any remark about the reactions is recorded, such as failure to carry out the initial instructions, hesitancy, misunderstanding of the stimulus words, such as 'bake' for 'cake,' phrases or exclamations instead of words, and so on.

The results are then collected and arranged in the form given below:

Reaction Times	*Frequency*	*Integrated Frequencies*	
·4	2	2	
·5	3	5	Number of faults=
·6	6	11	Number of failures=
etc.	etc.	etc.	

From this table it is easy to calculate the median (Mi), the quartile deviation (Q) and the coefficient of variability (C). The reaction times for all the subjects are pooled together and the ogive curve is drawn.

The following irregularities in reactions are said by Jung to be indicators of 'complexes:' (1) A reaction-word which is a repetition of the stimulus word; (2) faults; (3) failures; (4) perservations, i.e. the same reaction-word frequently given to different stimulus words; (5) prolonged reaction times, i.e. times which are more than 20 Q (say) above the median time. The 'complex' may be investigated by what is known as the 'free association' method, which technical term simply means that the subject is to talk at large about the words to which he has given the above irregular replies, without any reservations whatever.

ASSOCIATION WORDS

1. head
2. green
3. water
4. sing
5. dead
6. long
7. ship
8. make
9. woman
10. friendly
11. bake
12. ask
13. cold
14. stalk
15. dance
16. village
17. pond
18. sick
19. pride
20. bring
21. ink
22. angry
23. needle
24. swim
25. go
26. blue
27. lamp
28. carry
29. bread
30. rich
31. tree
32. jump
33. pity
34. yellow
35. street
36. bury
37. salt
38. new
39. habit
40. pray
41. money
42. silly
43. book
44. despise
45. finger
46. jolly
47. bird
48. walk
49. paper
50. wicked
51. frog
52. try
53. hunger
54. white
55. child
56. speak
57. pencil
58. sad
59. plum
60. marry
61. home
62. nasty
63. glass
64. fight
65. wool
66. big
67. carrot
68. give
69. doctor
70. frosty
71. flower
72. beat
73. box
74. old
75. family
76. wait
77. cow
78. name
79. luck
80. say
81. table
82. naughty
83. brother
84. afraid
85. love
86. chair
87. worry
88. kiss
89. bride
90. clean
91. bag
92. choice
93. bed
94. pleased
95. happy
96. shut
97. wound
98. evil
99. door
100. insult

For a discussion of this topic and results see the author's *Educational Psychology*, Ch. IX.

Preference

Experiment 16

The purpose of this experiment is to study the effect of subjective preference on memory. It is often assumed that efficiency in memory depends on the method by which the material is memorised. This experiment is designed to discover whether preference for what is learnt can override the method of learning.

The class is divided into subjects and experimenters, and each subject learns two sonnets by the same author. Thus four sonnets altogether are required, and they should be as similar in conception as possible. (The four sonnets by Thomas Hardy printed in his collected poems and called *She to Him* are suitable).

The first sonnet is learnt by the 'entire' method, i.e. by reading through the whole from beginning to end eight times with a pause of about one minute between the readings. A minute after the final reading the experimenter hears his subject recite the sonnet and makes a record of the number of times he has to prompt him during the recitation. A convenient method is to underline the places of prompting on a typed copy of the poem. For this purpose prepositions, articles and conjunctions may be ignored.

The second sonnet is learnt by the 'sectional' method of breaking it up into three parts: the two quatrains and the sestette. Hence it is necessary to choose poems with strong punctuation marks at these points, which is often the case. The scheme of repetitions is as follows:

	Repetitions		
First quatrain	4	2	2
Second quatrain	4		
Sestette		6	

This is, the first quatrain is repeated four times; then the second four times. Then the whole octave is repeated twice, after which the sestette is repeated six times, and then the whole sonnet is repeated twice. In this way each line has been repeated exactly eight times, i.e. as frequently as the first sonnet. There should be a pause of about one minute after each section. A minute after the final reading the poem is recited to the experimenter, who scores the prompts, as before.

In order to arouse interest and diminish fatigue, subjects and experimenters exchange rôles after each poem has been recited. When the experiment is finished the subjects are asked to state which of the two sonnets they prefer, and preferences are recorded.

A week later each poem is read through a single time from start to finish, and the number of prompts is recorded precisely as before; the subjects having previously been told to avoid thinking about them in the interval.

Tables are now drawn up in the form here shown:

NUMBER OF PROMPTS.

	Immediate Recall		Delayed Recall	
	Sonnet I	*Sonnet II*	*Sonnet I*	*Sonnet II*
Subjects				
A				
B				
C				
D				

These data are next reclassified in accordance with the preference of the subject, and the average number of prompts for each group is recorded thus:

MEAN NUMBER OF PROMPTS.

	Immediate Recall		Delayed Recall	
	Sonnet I	*Sonnet II*	*Sonnet I*	*Sonnet II*
Subjects preferring Sonnet I				
Subjects preferring Sonnet II				
No preference				

For a full discussion of the results see the *British Journal of Psychology*, vol. xiii., 1923, article by C. Fox on "Influence of Subjective Preference on Memory."

Logical Memory

Experiment 17

The purpose of this experiment is to study rational memory or the memory for logical ideas. Most so-called experiments on memory are really concerned with the study of the formation of vocal habits, and the present experiment is designed to avoid this pitfall, as far as may be. The extract to be memorised is from Berkeley's *Principles of Human Knowledge* and contains twenty sharply defined ideas presented in a logical order.

The division into separate ideas is indicated in the text. The text may be used with the dividing lines, or it may be typed with these omitted, but in the latter case the experiment is more difficult as the lines help the subject to organise his reading.

Each subject reads through the piece carefully at his own rate from beginning to end, and is told that he may and should read sentences again where they are not clear to him. When he has finished he takes a rest for about two or three minutes and then reads the extract through again, and after a similar interval repeats the reading a third time. The subject is instructed that he should follow the train of thought and make no conscious attempt to remember the exact phraseology.

After a further interval of two or three minutes, filled up by irrelevant conversation, the subject writes out all he can recollect of the thought of the passage in his own words. The experimenter marks the papers by giving a mark to each thought correctly reproduced. No attention whatever is given to the phraseology in which the thought is expressed, provided that the substance is correct.

The subject is told to dismiss the passages from his mind, and a week later he is again asked to reproduce the substance of the extract.

A comparison may thus be made of the variations in immediate and delayed reproduction, and introspective data should be furnished by the subject.

An examination of the scripts will show whether there has been any reminiscent activity during the week. If so, the amount of absolute and relative reminiscence should be calculated. By relative reminiscence is meant the ratio of the number of ideas originally forgotten, but now remembered, to the number originally remembered.

Extract from Berkeley

It is evident to any one who takes a survey of the objects of human knowledge, that they are either ideas actually imprinted on the senses; | or else such as are perceived by attending to the passions and operations of the mind; | or lastly, ideas formed by help of memory and imagination—either compounding, dividing, or barely representing those originally perceived in the aforesaid ways. | By sight I have the ideas of light and colours, with their several degrees and variations. By touch I perceive hard and soft, heat and cold, motion and resistance, and of all these more or less either as to quantity or degree. Smelling furnishes me with odours; the palate with tastes; and hearing conveys sounds to the mind in all their variety of tone and composition. | And as several of these are observed to accompany each other, they come to be marked by one name, and so to be reputed as one thing. | Thus, for example, a certain colour, taste, smell, figure and consistence having been observed to go together, are accounted one distinct thing, signified by the name apple; other collections of ideas constitute a stone, a tree, a book, and the like sensible things | —which as they are pleasing or disagreeable excite the passions of love, hatred, joy, grief, and so forth. |

That neither our thoughts, nor passions, nor ideas formed by the imagination, exist without the mind, is what everybody will allow. | And to me it is no less evident that the various sensations or ideas imprinted on the sense, however blended or combined together (that is, whatever objects they compose), cannot exist otherwise than in a mind perceiving them. | I think an intuitive knowledge may be obtained of this by any one that shall attend to what is meant by the term exist when applied to sensible things. | The table I write on I say exists, that is, I see and feel it; | and if it were out of my study I should say it existed—meaning thereby that if I was in my study I might perceive it, or that some other spirit actually does perceive it. | There was an odour, that is, it was smelt; there was a sound, that is, it was heard; a colour or figure, and it was perceived by sight or touch. This is all that I can understand by these and the like expressions. | For as to what is said of the absolute existence of unthinking things without any relation to their being perceived, that is to me perfectly unintelligible. | Their *esse* is *percipi*, nor is it possible they should have any existence out of the minds or thinking things which perceive them. |

It is indeed an opinion strangely prevailing amongst men, that houses, mountains, rivers, and in a word all sensible objects have an existence, natural or real, distinct from their being perceived by the understanding. | But, with how great an assurance and acquiescence soever this principle may be entertained in the world, yet whoever shall find in his heart to call it in question may, if I mistake not, perceive it to involve a manifest contradiction. | For, what are the forementioned objects but things we perceive by sense ? and what do we perceive besides our own ideas or sensations ? and is it not plainly repugnant that any one of these, or any combination of them, should exist unperceived ? |

But, say you, though the ideas themselves do not exist without the mind, yet there may be things like them, whereof they are copies or resemblances, which things exist without the mind in an unthinking substance. | I answer, an idea can be like nothing but an idea; a colour or figure can be like nothing but another colour or figure. |

Reminiscence

Experiment 18

An attempt is made in this experiment to discover whether individual subjects display any reminiscent activity in memorising.

The passage chosen is from Coleridge and the number of repetitions suggested is based on experiments with adults. The passage is memorised by reading it through fourteen times, slowly and deliberately. After this a rest is taken, at the end of which the subjects write out all they can remember. The experimenter marks the sheets on the following plan: Only whole lines reproduced, without gaps, are counted as correct. Errors in prepositions, articles, conjunctions, relative pronouns are ignored; as also such slight errors as 'hill' for 'slope,' 'quiet' for 'silent,' etc., the principle being that purely verbal errors are ignored, provided that the sense is correctly reproduced.

The subjects are now divided into three or more groups; each group containing equal numbers of good and bad memorisers as determined by the number of lines correctly reproduced. They are instructed to dismiss the lines from their thoughts in the intervening period. At intervals of one, two or three days, etc., the different groups reproduce, in writing, all they can, and the number of correct lines is calculated as before.

It is now a simple matter to calculate the amount of reminiscence and obliviscence for each period of time. By the amount of reminiscence is meant the number of lines correctly reproduced which were not reproduced correctly immediately after learning. Obliviscence is the failure to reproduce lines correctly written after learning. The quantities of reminiscence should be calculated both absolutely and relatively. Relative reminiscence is determined by finding the percentage of recovered lines compared with the total number immediately reproduced after learning.

An instructive experiment may be made by trying this experiment on school children and comparing the results with those obtained from adults. In this way it may be determined whether absolute or relative reminiscence diminishes with maturity.

EXTRACT FROM COLERIDGE.

A green and silent spot, amid the hills,
A small and silent dell! O'er stiller place
No singing sky-lark ever poised himself.

The hills are heathy, save that swelling slope,
Which hath a gay and gorgeous covering on,
All golden with the never-bloomless furze,
Which now blooms most profusely: but the dell,
Bathed by the mist, is fresh and delicate
As vernal corn-field, or the unripe flax,
When, through its half-transparent stalks, at eve,
The level sunshine glimmers with green light.
Oh! 'tis a quiet spirit-healing nook!
Which all, methinks, would love; but chiefly he
The humble man, who, in his youthful years,
Knew just so much of folly, as had made
His early manhood more securely wise!
Here he might lie on fern or withered heath,
While from the singing lark (that sings unseen
The minstrelsy that solitude loves best),
And from the sun, and from the breezy air,
Sweet influences trembled o'er his frame;
And he, with many feelings, many thoughts,
Made up a meditative joy and found
Religious meanings in the forms of Nature!
And so, his senses gradually wrapt
In a half sleep, he dreams of better worlds,
And dreaming hears thee still, O singing lark,
That singest like an angel in the clouds.

For discussion of results see "Reminiscence and Obliviscence," in *British Journal of Psychology*, Monograph Supplement, vol. i., No. 2, by Ballard.

CHAPTER V

SUGGESTION

Directing Ideas

Experiment 19

The object of the following two experiments is to trace and measure the influence of a ' directing idea ' in suggestion. The directions here given are intended for a group of subjects, and it must be borne in mind that in all experiments on suggestion it is essential to follow the directions with the most minute care, as the slightest deviation makes a difference in the suggestive effects. The apparatus to be used is shown here, but any other method of displaying lines of varying known length may be employed. It consists of a ruler on the back of which a strip of white paper has been pasted with a black line 1 mm. thick running all the way down the centre. The ruler slides into a slotted wooden case, lined with felt to prevent slipping, and the back of the case is covered with black paper (see p. 94). Each subject is provided with a sheet of squared paper.

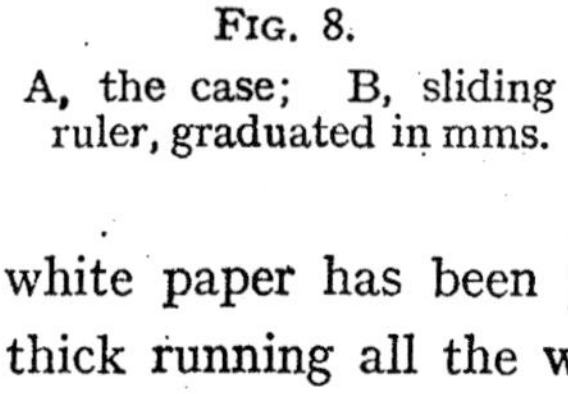

FIG. 8.
A, the case; B, sliding ruler, graduated in mms.

The experimenter stands 6 feet in front of the group of subjects behind a screen which covers his hands so that he may manipulate the sliding ruler without the latter being seen by the subjects. The subjects are instructed to record the lengths of the lines shown to them by making a cross on the squared paper representing the height of the line above the base. They should previously draw a thick line to represent the base and at intervals of 1 cm. write the numbers from 1 to 12. The length of each line is to be recorded by a cross vertically above its corresponding number. When the numbers have been written the experimenter gives the following instructions exactly as printed:

"We are going to try an experiment on vision, to see how well you can judge the length of a line. I shall show you some lines, one after the other, and you will reproduce them immediately afterwards. In this way I shall be able to tell how well you have judged their length by sight. There are some people whose vision is so bad that if I show them a line of 5 cms. (here show this line) they reproduce one of 10 cms. (show this length), others produce one of 2 cms. (show this). I want you to do your best and draw exactly what you see."

When this formula has been given, the experimenter asks whether the instructions have been understood and gives any further explanation. The ruler is adjusted behind the screen and the following vertical lines are shown in order, the lengths being read off on the face of the ruler.

12, 24, 36, 48, 60, *60*, 72, *72*, 84, *84*, 96, *96* mms.

The lines are shown, vertically, above the screen, always at the same height and each for 5 seconds. Care should be taken to have a neutral background so that the lengths may not be judged by reference to this, and for the same reason the ruler is held far away from the body. Before showing each line the experimenter says: "Ready! Here's another line!" No question should be answered during the progress of the experiment, which should proceed rapidly, but the experimenter should watch to see that all the subjects have recorded their lengths before the next line is shown.

There are 4 'trap' lines in the series and a coefficient of suggestibility may be calculated by the help of these. The mean increase in length made by a subject in the 4 'trap' lines is calculated, i.e. the increase from line 5 to line 6, 7 to 8, 9 to 10, and 11 to 12. Call this mean Ms. The mean increase shown in the lines 4 to 5, 6 to 7, 8 to 9, 10 to 11 is also measured. Call this Mp.

Then the coefficient of suggestibility,

$$K = \frac{Ms}{Mp} \times 100.$$

By this coefficient the subjects may be 'ranked.'

Experiment 20

This experiment is a variant of the preceding and gives some qualitative information not yielded by the former. It gives more satisfactory results.

The apparatus and procedure are exactly as before. Having arranged all the preliminaries and having instructed the subjects to mark the base line and insert the numbers, this time from 1 to 20, the experimenter makes the following statement: "We are going to try the same experiment as before, but this time there will be 20 lines. Be sure that you show the lengths of the lines correctly now that you have had some practice." Or this experiment may be tried without the preliminary experiment, in which case the previous instructions must be given.

The 20 lines to be shown are of the following lengths in cms.:

2, 4, 6, 8, 10, 12, 14, 14, 14, etc.

the last 14 lines being of the same length. The coefficient of suggestibility is calculated thus:

$$K = \frac{\text{length of the longest line drawn}}{\text{length of 7th line}} \times 100.$$

The subjects may thus be 'ranked,' and if the previous experiment has been performed the correlation coefficient between the two sets of ranks may be worked out.

When the records are collected the subjects may be classified into the following types: (1) The non-suggestible

—those who resist the suggestion completely or recover brusquely shortly after the 8th line, making all the rest equal or approximately so. (2) The hesitant types—(*a*) who act on the suggestion for some time and then correct themselves somewhat but never sufficiently to throw off the suggestion. (*b*) Those who continue to carry out the suggestion till the end, but whose increments get smaller and smaller after a certain point. (3) The automatic type who act on the suggestion all through the series, the increments being the same all the time. These are completely suggestible. (4) The rhythmic type—those who correct themselves brusquely after a time, then again carry out the suggestion, and again correct themselves, and so on through the last 14 lines. Varieties of this type are also to be observed in the three preceding types.

The subjects of the last three types are then interrogated by the following questionnaire, and their replies written down:

(*a*) Do you think your lines are right?

(*b*) Have you made any mistakes?

(*c*) Have you made any of your lines too short or too long? If he says he has made them too long ask him to correct them by making small circles to indicate the correct lengths. When he has finished proceed thus:

(*d*) How did you know you had made them too long?

(*e*) When did you see that you had made them too long?

(*f*) Why did you go on making them too long after you saw you were wrong?

These questions may be more colloquial so as to gain the confidence of the subject, who must not receive the impression that he is being cross-examined, but simply interrogated out of curiosity.

For a discussion of results see *La Suggestibilité*, by A. Binet, published by Schleicher Frères, Paris, 1900.

Personal Suggestion

Experiment 21

In the previous experiments on suggestion the personality of the experimenter was, as it were, in the background. The object of the present experiment is to test and measure suggestibility when the personal factor is prominent.

For this purpose six pictures are used (see Appendix IV.). If the experiment is performed with a group of subjects the pictures may be made into lantern slides. Each picture is shown for 10 seconds by a stop watch.

The subjects are provided with a sheet of paper divided as below on which they write their replies.

SUBJECT : EXPERIMENTER : DATE :

Number of Picture	*Question* 1	*Question* 2	*Are you Certain of your Replies ?*	*Uncertainty due to*	*Comments*	*Revision*
			1. 2.			

Before the pictures are shown the experimenter reads the following instructions in a firm voice: "The pictures you will be shown are to test the accuracy of your observation. You will have adequate time for observation and you should observe carefully. After each picture has been withdrawn, I will ask you simple questions about it, which you will answer on the sheets in front of you. Are you ready? Now!"

After the picture has been withdrawn the subjects write its number in the first column. The first question is then asked and answered: and then the second. The experimenter then asks: "Are you certain of your replies?" and the subjects write 'Yes' or 'No' for each question in the appropriate column. The next two columns are then filled in, but the final column is left vacant until the end of the whole experiment. When all the pictures have been exhibited the experimenter says: "Revise your answers, if you wish, in the last column. I do not want you to adhere to your original replies if you desire to change them, but do not cross out what you have written. If you do revise an answer state briefly the reason for your previous incorrect reply."

The following are the questions to be asked with reference to each picture:

(1) The picture shows a riverside.

1. Do you remember the windmill?
2. How many sails had it?

(2)

1. Did he look like a student or a tradesman?
2. Was he wearing a stand-up or a lay-down collar?

(3)
1. What was the nationality of the artist ?
2. What was the shape of his palette ?

(4)
1. What do you think was this man's profession ?
2. How many buttons, approximately, had he on his waistcoat ?

(5)
1. Do you remember the two chimney stacks ?
2. How many chimney pots, approximately, on each ?

(6)
1. What sort of collar was he wearing ?
2. Had he a monocle or an eyeglass ?

The scoring is done on the following scheme:

2 marks for being trapped.
1 for certainty of answer.
1 for incorrect revision.
−1 for uncertainty of answer (if wrong).
−1 for correct revision (of wrong answer).

It is thus possible to secure 3 marks on each picture, making a total of 18 for complete suggestibility. The number of marks obtained may be regarded as an index of suggestibility.

The correlation coefficient for these indices and the coefficient of suggestibility in the previous experiment may be worked out. As the two experiments are so widely different, especially in the personal factor, the result will probably approximate to zero.

The following table shows the frequency-distribution of the indices for sixty-three University graduates:

Index ..	0	1	2	3	4	5	6	7	8	9	10	11	12
Number ..	7	9	6	9	8	11	4	2	2	0	1	2	2

CHAPTER VI

REASONING AND KNOWLEDGE TESTS

Tests of Reasoning

Experiment 22

This test has been drawn up so as to be suitable for adult students, and the varieties of reasoning tested are very diverse. The great objection to most mental tests is that none is sufficiently difficult to put adults on their mettle. This test has been proved, in practice, to get over this difficulty, and is given below.

No time limit is set, but it will be found that most honours graduates can do all that they are able in half an hour. The instruction given is that the answers, which should be written, must be as brief as possible.

In no case should an answer consist of more than a few sentences. Every question must be attempted, and in case of failure to answer the number of the question should be written, with a stroke to indicate the attempt.

Tests of Reasoning.

1. On taking an impression from a piece of mother-of-pearl in beeswax, balsam, fusible metal, lead, isinglass, and a large variety of other substances, it is always found that the iridescent colours are reproduced in these substances.

What can you infer from this as to the cause of the iridescence of mother-of-pearl ?

You may assume that nothing is rubbed off the mother-of-pearl.

2. 1,000 children were examined: 45 had bodily defects, 23 had nervous symptoms, 14 were mentally deficient.

Can we infer from these figures that any children with nervous symptoms are mentally deficient ?

If you think we can, say 'Yes.'

If you think we cannot, give a reason.

3. The following argument has been used to prove Newton's laws of motion: The times of eclipses are calculated by assuming Newton's laws to be true. The calculated times always agree with the observed times, consequently the laws must be true.

If this reasoning is *formally* sound, write 'Yes.'

If it is not, give a reason.

4. What conclusion can be *rigorously* drawn from the following propositions ? All the students of X College in the University during 1920 knew French or Russian, but not both; and in the University that year all who knew Russian were members of X College. There are eighteen colleges in the University.

5. The only proof capable of being given that an object is visible is that people actually see it. The only proof that a sound is audible is that people hear it; and so of the other sources of our experience. In like manner, the sole evidence it is possible to produce that anything is desirable, is that people do actually desire it.

If this argument is valid, write 'Yes.'

If it is not, give a reason.

6. The following rules were drawn up for a club:

(1) The financial Committee shall be chosen from amongst the General Committee.

(2) No one shall be a member both of the general and library Committees, unless he be also on the financial Committee.

(3) No member of the library Committee shall be on the financial Committee.

Is anything superfluous in these rules ?

If not, say 'No.'

If anything is superfluous, state what it is.

7. It has been argued that we have reason to believe in 'uniformities of nature,' i.e. to know that the future will resemble the past on the ground of experience because what was the future has constantly become the past, so that we really have experience of the future, namely, of times which were formerly future.

If this is sound, write 'Yes.'

If it is unsound, give a reason.

8. No reason can be given why the general happiness is desirable, except that each person, so far as he believes it to be attainable, desires his own happiness. If this latter statement is assumed as a fact, then each person's happiness is a good to that person, and the general happiness, therefore, a good to the aggregate of all persons.

If this reasoning is sound, write 'Yes.'

If it is not, give a reason.

Discussion of Results.—The diagram given in Part II. shows the distribution of the marks obtained by 140 graduates, mostly honours men, on this reasoning test.

The test was given to 58 pupils in the top form of four public schools, the age range of the pupils being from 16½ to 19 years. The distribution of the marks in the case was:

Marks	0	½–1	1½–2	2½–3	3½–4	4½–5	5½–6
Number of pupils ..	1	8	17	16	10	5	1

It is instructive to compare the average marks for each question of the graduates and the schoolboys.

Question	1	2	3	4	5	6	7	8	Mean
Graduates	0·51	0·72	0·20	0·20	0·45	0·25	0·26	0·30	2·9
Pupils	0·60	0·60	0·12	0·10	0·39	0·28	0·13	0·20	2·5

The general opinion amongst those who employ mental tests is that intelligence ceases to grow at about the age of 16 years. The questions in our tests are sufficiently difficult to put the persons on their mettle; and it will be seen that nobody gets more than 6 marks out of a maximum 8. The graduates obtained 16 per cent. more marks than the schoolboys, a result which shows that

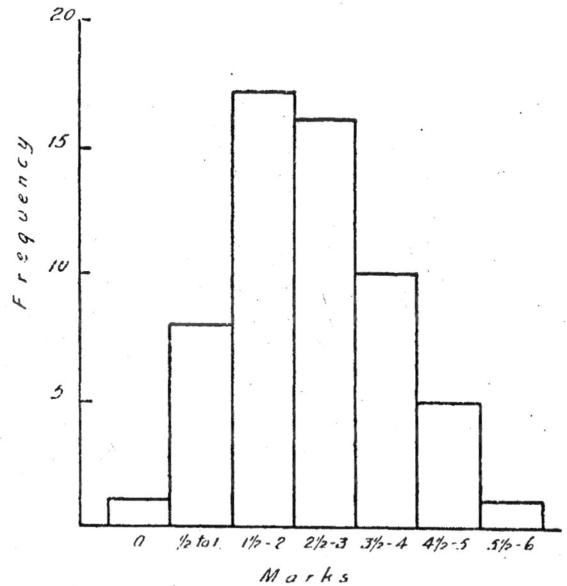

FIG. 9.—REASONING ABILITY OF SCHOOLBOYS (58 SUBJECTS).

reasoning ability does not cease to grow at the age of 16 or even 19. Mental tests, as a rule, are much too easy to interest the intelligent adult or to stimulate him to do his best. Another thing is obscured by ordinary mental tests, which is well brought out by these reasoning tests. The manner of tackling a test makes all the difference to the value of the answer. Two replies may both be correct and get full marks, yet one may be incomparably superior to the other in reasoning value; it is as we say, 'much neater' or 'prettier.' The kind of test which is answered by underlining alternatives completely ignores this qualitative difference of answers.

Solutions to these Reasoning tests are given in Appendix V.

Tests of General Knowledge

Experiment 23

The tests printed below are given on a typed sheet and the subjects are instructed to reply in writing in brief catalogue form, giving in a sentence or two only such information as is necessary to show that they know what the questions mean, or are acquainted with the facts or theories asked.

The marking should not be too pedantic. One mark is given for each question correctly answered. The replies to all the questions may be found in Webster's *New International Dictionary*, and these should be regarded as norms in marking. The notes in Appendix VI. indicate the kind of exactness required, but any reply which shows that the subject has *definite* familiarity with what is asked should be accepted.

This test has been given to 36 honours graduates, with the following results. The table shows the total marks obtained by the whole group for each set of questions. The average mark is 18·3.

Literature	*Philosophy*	*History*	*Geography*	*Law*	*Business*	*Politics*
55	51	66	41	13	69	70

Science	*Mythology*	*Medicine*	*Miscellaneous*	*Quotations*	*Synonyms*
57	55	22	50	49	63

The test should be given to school children and the norms compared.

TEST OF GENERAL KNOWLEDGE

LITERATURE

In which of Shakespeare's plays does Falstaff appear ?
Who was Mr. Mantalini ? Who is 'Mrs. Grundy' ?
For what was the 'Mermaid Tavern' famous ?
What is the story of 'Everyman' ? Who was 'Mrs. Malaprop' ?

PHILOSOPHY

What is the doctrine of Metempsychosis ? Who were the Utilitarians ?
What are the essentials of Darwin's theory ? What does metaphysics deal with ?
What did Plato mean by an Idea ? What are the doctrines of Bergson ?

HISTORY

What is the historical meaning of cabal ? Who was the Great Mogul ?
What was the Boston Tea Party ?
When was Pompeii destroyed ? Who were the Merchant Adventurers ?
What is meant by the Renaissance ?

GEOGRAPHY

What is a geographical mile? Where is the Iron Gate?
What is an isotherm? Where is the Murman Coast?
What are the Pillars of Hercules? What is the azimuth?

LAW

Explain 'caveat emptor.' What place in English law is filled by John Doe?
What is a writ of 'nisi prius'? What is compounding a felony?
What is a caveat? What is meant by the 'conflict of laws'?

BUSINESS TERMS

What is a demurrage? What is a bonded warehouse?
Which expenses are termed 'overhead charges'?
What is a letter of credit? What is the plimsoll mark?
Why is an underwriter so called?

POLITICS

What is a Soviet? In what year did Gladstone die?
What is the meaning of Bolshevik? What is Manchesterism?
What is the 'International'?
How did the word 'candidate' originate?

SCIENCE

What are the properties of radium? What is meant by the quantum theory?
What is the nebular hypothesis? What is an electron?
What is a hygrometer? What is the purpose of an induction coil?

MYTHOLOGY

What is the story of Prometheus? Who were the Titans?
What is the story of Dædalus and Icarus?
What was the punishment of Sisyphus?
What does Thor's hammer represent? Who was Prester John?

MEDICINE

What are the vitamines ? On what theory is psycho-analysis based ?
What is Pasteurism ? What are the characteristic symptoms of small-pox ?
Name the bones of the arm ? What are ductless glands ?

MISCELLANEOUS

What is the Rosetta stone ? When is a sailing-vessel close-hauled ?
Why are German submarines called U-boats ? What is pinchbeck ?
Why was a grocer originally so called ? What is a Cheshire cat ?

QUOTATIONS

What is the meaning of the following phrases:

Fait accompli. Persona grata. Tertium quid.
Verbum sap. Apropos de bottes. Dolce far niente.

SYNONYMS

In what respects do the following words differ in meaning:

Egoism and egotism. Covetous and avaricious.
Liberal and generous. Irony and sarcasm.
Laziness and idleness. Solicitude and anxiety.

CHAPTER VII

APPRECIATION TESTS

Literary Appreciation

Experiment 24

The purpose of this experiment is twofold: (*a*) to get some measure of the relative ability of different persons in the appreciation of literature; (*b*) to analyse the various factors involved in such appreciation.

(*a*) The nine selections on p. 84 are given to the subjects, together with the instructions which are typed on a separate slip. It is desirable to impress the instructions ve[illegible]y, more especially the necessity of assigning each extract to its appropriate category *independently* of the others, and to state clearly that numbers only should be written on the slip. Whilst each poem is being read, the others should be covered and dismissed from the mind.

If the subject asks for further information he should be told that what is wanted is the worth or value of each selection considered by itself *as poetry*.

The instructions are:

"Read through each poem carefully six times. Then with the following key in front of you assign to each, as well as you can, its position on the scale, graduating according to poetic merit. Be sure to treat each poem *alone*, without reference to any of the other extracts.

1. First rate.
2. Good.
3. Medium.
4. Indifferent.
5. Poor.

Write against this scale the number of the poem, but make no comments."

(*b*) The slips are collected, and the experimenter notes the classification. A second typed slip is now given to the subjects. In the blank spaces the experimenter inserts 4 numbers for each subject, two from those assigned to Grades 1 or 2, and two from Grades 4 and 5. Each subject, of course, being given those which he himself has assigned to these grades. The questions are answered with the appropriate poem in front of the subject for reference.

"With regard to ....,
state whether:

(*a*) You like, dislike, admire, or are in any other way affected by the poem.

(*b*) Whether you can assign any specific ground for this feeling; and state what it is.

(*c*) Was your original judgment on the poem due to the feeling (*a*) or the reason given in (*b*), or to any other cause? State precisely what determined the judgment.

(*d*) Did you in any case dislike a poem and yet give it a high rank, or like it and give it a low rank? Why?

Deal with each poem separately; and write on your sheets the number of the poem, and (*a*), (*b*), (*c*), and (*d*) in order. If you cannot give an answer to any of these sections, write the letter and pass to the next."

The method of marking is based on the opinion of certain experts, poets, and lecturers on English, to whom the nine extracts were submitted. They were asked to choose the 'best' and the 'worst,' and their consensus of opinion is taken as the standard. The four 'best' chosen by the votes of the experts were 2, 5, 6, 9, and the three 'worst' 3, 4, 7.

The poems not selected by the experts, i.e. 1 and 8, are to be ignored in marking. If a subject assigns a 'best' poem to the categories 1 or 2, he secures 2 marks, if to 3, he gets 0 marks, if to 4 he gets −1, and to 5 he gets −2. This order is exactly reversed for marking the 'worst' poems. The maximum mark for the whole series is therefore 14; and a subject's total may be negative.

Appreciation Tests

1.

" What merest whim
Seems all this poor endeavour after fame,
To one who keeps within his steadfast aim
A love immortal, an immortal too.
Look not so wildered; for these things are true

And never can be born of atomies
That buzz about our slumbers like brain flies,
Leaving us fancy-sick. No, No, I'm sure,
My restless spirit never could endure
To brood so long upon one luxury,
Unless it did, though fearfully, espy
A hope beyond the shadow of a dream."

2.

" I would rather be struck dumb
Than speak against this ardent listlessness:
For I have ever thought that it might bless
The world with benefits unknowingly;
As does the nightingale up-perched high
And cloister'd among cool and bunched leaves—
She sings but to her love, nor e'er conceives
How tiptoe Night holds back her dark grey hood."

3.

" Ah, thou wilt steal
Away from me again, indeed, indeed—
Thou wilt be gone away and wilt not heed
My lonely madness. Speak my kindest fair !
Is—is it to be so ? No ! Who will dare
To pluck thee from me ? And of thine own will,
Full well I feel thou wouldst not leave me. Still
Let me entwine thee surer, surer—now
How can we part ? Elysium ! Who art thou ?
Who, that thou canst not be for ever here,
Or lift me with thee to some starry sphere ?"

4.

" There are who lord it o'er their fellow men
With most prevailing tinsel: who unpen
Their baaing vanities, to browse away
The comfortable green and juicy hay

From human pastures; or, O torturing fact!
Who, through an idiot blink, will see unpack'd
Fire-branded foxes to sear up and singe
Our old and ripe ear'd hopes. With not one tinge
Of sanctuary splendour, not a sight
Able to face an owl's, they still are dight
By the blear-eyed nations in empurpled vests
And crowns and turbans."

5.

" 'Tis the grot
Of Proserpine, when Hell, obscure and hot,
Doth her resign; and where her tender hands
She dabbles on the cool and sluicy sands.
Or 'tis the cell of Echo, where she sits,
And bubbles thorough silence, till her wits
Are gone in tender madness, and anon,
Faints into sleep, with many a dying tone
Of sadness."

6.

" Rain-scented eglantine
Gave temperate sweets to that well-wooing sun:
The lark was lost in him; cold springs had run
To warm their chilliest bubbles in the grass;
Man's voice was on the mountains; and the mass
Of nature's lives and wonders pulsed tenfold,
To feel this sun-rise and its glories old."

7.

" Now, is it not a shame
To see ye thus—not very, very sad?
Perhaps ye are too happy to be glad:
O feel as if it were a common day;
Free voiced as one who never was away.

No tongue shall ask, whence come ye ? but ye shall
Be gods of your own rest imperial.
Not even I, for one whole month, will pry
Into the hours that have passed us by,
Since in my arbour I did sing to thee."

8.

" When the airy stress
Of music's kiss impregnates the free winds,
And with a sympathetic touch unbinds
Æolian magic from their lucid wombs;
The old songs waken from enclouded tombs;
Old ditties sigh above their father's grave;
Ghosts of melodious prophesyings rave
Round every spot where trod Apollo's foot;
Bronze clarions awake, and faintly bruit,
Where long ago a giant battle was;
And, from the turf, a lullaby doth pass
In every place where infant Orpheus slept."

9.

" Ah, 'tis the thought,
The deadly feel of solitude: for lo !
He cannot see the heavens, nor the flow
Of rivers, nor hill flowers running wild
In pink and purple chequer, nor, up-piled
The cloudy rack slow journeying in the west
Like herded elephants; nor felt nor prest
Cool grass, nor tasted the fresh slumberous air,
But far from such companionship to wear
An unknown time, surcharged with grief away,
Was now his lot."

Discussion of Results.—This test has been tried on 156 graduates (95 men and 61 women), and the distribution of marks is shown in the accompanying diagram.

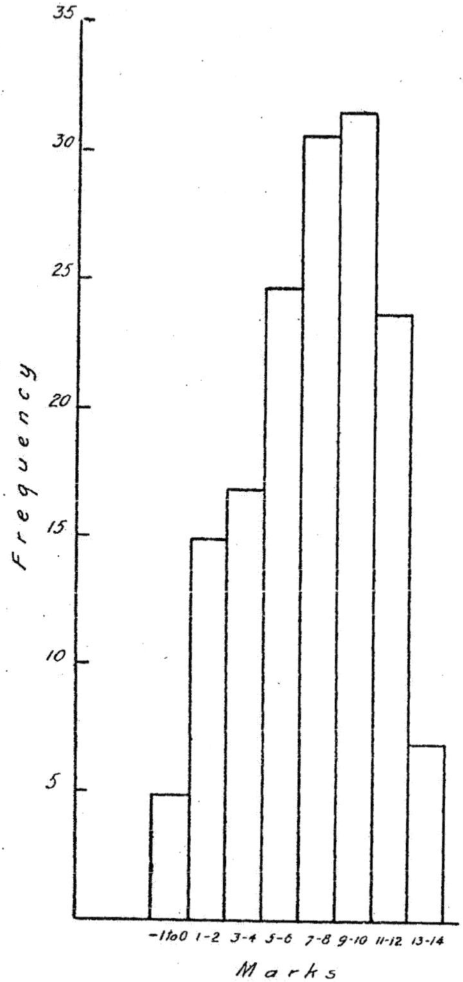

FIG. 10.—DISTRIBUTION OF LITERARY APPRECIATION (156 subjects: 95 men, 61 women).

The diagram suggests that the capacity for literary appreciation is not symmetrically distributed.

The second part of the experiment provides a means of research by which the various factors which influence appreciation may be disentangled. It should be borne in mind in such an investigation that there is no necessary connection between the feelings aroused by a work of art and its appreciation. Some persons, for instance, may assign a very low rank to a poem, not on account of any active dislike, but because they discern no merit or import in it; and, on the other hand, intense enjoyment of a sensuous kind may be derived, whilst nevertheless the poem would not be ranked high in the scale.

The subjects whose record is displayed in the diagram gave a high rank to the extracts for the following main reasons: appropriateness or smoothness of the rhythm, the music of the verse, aptness or beauty of the descriptions, rhymes, the suitability of the epithets or adjectives, beauty of the language including metaphor and simile, etc. The emotional or subjective factors which favoured a high rank were mystical feelings aroused, contrast of fact and fancy, the sentiment suggested or a deep emotion. stirred; and allied with these, the vividness and relevancy of the imagery fusing with and colouring the emotion Other factors were the associations suggested by the poems, the delicacy or attractiveness of the word pictures, etc. Finally, the appreciation rested on the simplicity and delicacy of the expressions themselves apart from their associated images; and the vigour, truth, or appropriateness of the language to express the feelings conveyed.

A low rank was assigned for a variety of reasons: rhythm or rhymes bad or faulty, expressions forced or obscure, epithets inappropriate, metaphors strained or high flown. The triviality of the thoughts and insincerity of the sentiments or the feelings were constant reasons for ranking an extract low in the scale. Failure to understand the piece fully produced the same result. Sometimes the sensuous nature of the poem or the shallowness of the emotions or gross sentimentality produced the same result. The whole subject of the analysis of the factors producing appreciation or its opposite stands in need of much further investigation.

The selections were all made from Keats' *Endymion* but this is not stated to the subjects. At the end of the experiment they may be told that the poems are all by the same author, and they are to guess the name.

It is interesting to compare the results in these tests with the academic subjects studied by the students. A group of sixty-six graduates were tested, and were classified into four classes of merit on the basis of the tests. The subjects studied by them were also classified into four groups: Classics or English, Modern Languages, History, Science or Mathematics. A 4×4 fold contingency table was constructed from these data. The mean square contingency coefficient was found to be $C = \cdot 25$ (the maximum coefficient for a 4×4 fold table is $\cdot 87$).

Musical Appreciation

Experiment 25

The purpose of this experiment is to compare the relative ability of different persons in the capacity for musical appreciation.

The twelve gramophone records, described below, are played under concert-room conditions by the experimenter, and the task of the subjects consists in judging whether each is good or poor. They were chosen by a musical expert in such a manner that each 'good' selection contains a beautiful 'musical thought.' The first six records are by the same composer and the second six by different composers. All the records are those called 'His Master's Voice,' except No. 7, which is a Parlophone record. Only a part of each record is played, and the last column in the table indicates the part chosen; thus 0–$\frac{1}{4}$ implies that the first quarter is played, $\frac{1}{6}$–$\frac{1}{3}$ means that you start at $\frac{1}{6}$th from the beginning and stop at $\frac{1}{3}$rd from the beginning, and so on. Each subject has a sheet of paper before him ruled as on p. 92.

The following instructions are given verbally or printed: "The first six records are by one composer; and the second six by different composers. You are required to give your opinion of the records, regarded solely from the standpoint of musical worth, by putting a cross in the appropriate column. Do not compare them with each other, but judge each by itself."

SUBJECT: EXPERIMENTER: DATE:

	Record	*Good*	*Poor*
Test I.	1 2 3 4 5 6		
Test II.	1 2 3 4 5 6		

Each record is played through twice, and after the second time the subject records his judgment.

	No.	*Good*	*Poor*	*Record*	*Part Played*
I.				The first 6 records are from *Symphonie Fantastique*, Op. 4. Berlioz.	
	1	G		*Rêveries passion*—3rd record	$\frac{1}{6}$-$\frac{1}{3}$
	2		B	*Un bal*—1st record	$\frac{1}{4}$-$\frac{1}{3}$
	3	G		*Rêveries passion*—1st record	0-$\frac{1}{3}$
	4		B	*Scène aux champs*—2nd record	0-$\frac{1}{4}$
	5		B	*Songe d'une nuit de Sabbat*—1st record	0-$\frac{1}{4}$
	6	G		*Rêveries passion*—2nd record	0-$\frac{1}{3}$
II.					
	7	G		Wagner, *Tristan and Isolde.* Introd. to Act I. Part I. Parlophone record E. 10390	$\frac{3}{4}$-end
	8		B	Liszt, *Hungarian Rhapsody No.* 2. D. 144	$\frac{2}{3}$-end
	9	G		Byrd, *Fantazia for String Sextet.* Part II. E. 293	0-$\frac{1}{3}$
	10		B	Mendelssohn, *On Wings of Song.* Red 2-07982	$\frac{3}{4}$-end
	11		B	Shipley, Douglas, *D'ye ken John Peel.* C. 402	$\frac{3}{4}$-end
	12	G		Bach, *Brandenburg Concerto No.* 3. D. 683	0-$\frac{1}{4}$

Two marks are given for a correct choice, 2 are subtracted for an incorrect choice. No information beyond that stated above is given. The table on p. 92 shows the correct choices, the description of the record, and the portion to be played.

Results.—The gramophone tests were tried on 34 University students. This particular group had attended a course of instruction in musical appreciation a year before the tests were given, and had undergone an examination on the course. On the basis of the marks of this examination they had been classified into 4 groups in order of merit, A_1, A_2, A_3, A_4. They were now classified on the basis of the tests, and again placed in 4 classes in order of merit, B_1, B_2, B_3, B_4.

The numbers are too small to warrant any exact deduction; but the following shows the contingency table:

EXAMINATION GROUPS

	A_1	A_2	A_3	A_4	*Total*
Test groups:					
B_1	3	2	2	0	7
B_2	2	6	4	0	12
B_3	3	1	2	3	9
B_4	1	1	2	2	6
Total..	9	10	10	5	34

The mean square contingency coefficient for this table is found to be $C = \cdot 50$. The maximum for such a 4×4 fold classification is ·87. The tests are therefore very satisfactory.

CHAPTER VIII

THE EFFECTS OF TRAINING

Estimating Lengths

Experiment 26

The problem which this experiment is designed to investigate has been traditionally called the problem of the 'transfer of training.' But this name is meaningless, and the question at issue is whether the effects of practice can be carried over into new spheres of activity, i.e. whether training is general or specific.

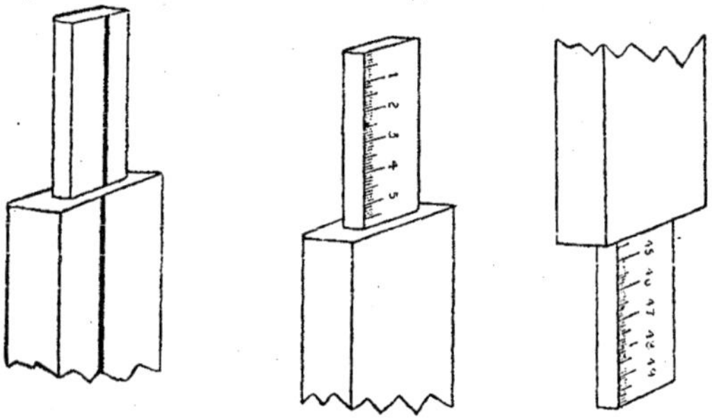

FIG. 11.

The apparatus to be used is that described in Experiment 19, but now both the back of the case and the back of the ruler are covered with white strips having a black line 1 mm. thick running down the centre of each. The object of this arrangement is to allow the simultaneous presentation of two lines, the standard and a variable.

The method to be employed consists in testing the ability of the subject to perform a certain task (the test series); then training him to perform a somewhat different task (the practice series); and finally testing his ability again in the original task.

Both the test series and the practice series in our experiment have been selected from the simplest material, in order to keep the essential feature of the problem as clear from complications as possible. The task of the subject is to 'produce' a line equal to a standard line chosen by the experimenter, and the method of determining this equivalence is called *the method of mean error.*

The class is divided into subjects and experimenters, and each tests the other. A standard line of 12 cms. (say) is selected as the standard length and should be the same for the whole class. This line is cut off on the back of the case by means of a strip of black paper adjusted to the proper length. A few preliminary trials should be given on a line of different length for the sake of accustoming the subject to the experimental conditions.

A series of 36 variable lines is presented successively by the experimenter to the subject, the variable being in every case *vertically* above the standard. Such a series should consist of groups of equal numbers of lines much shorter, much longer, moderately shorter and moderately longer than the standard. The subject is instructed to change the length of the variable so as to produce a line which appears equal to the standard. The apparatus is held by the subject at arm's length with the point of junction of the standard and variable lines opposite the centre of vision.

The crude average error is found from the readings and also the coefficient of variability. The former quantity gives a rough measure of the subject's accuracy, the latter of his consistency. Using either of these quantities, but preferably the latter, the class should be divided into two equivalent groups.

One group is now practised for a week, a series of readings being taken daily in the manner above described, but *horizontal* lines are now used, the standard being of the same length as before, i.e. 12 cms. At the end of each sitting, the subject is told whether he is better or worse than the preceding day, in order to stimulate him to do better.

Experiment 27

This experiment is the completion of the previous one. Both the practised and the unpractised groups are tested on estimating the length of the original standard *vertical* line. The average error or the coefficient of variability is used as the measure according to which of these has been employed in dividing the groups. Careful introspections are dictated by the subject to the experimenter so as to discover in what the improvement (if any) consists.

Both groups have had some initial practice on the vertical line and, therefore, if evidence of transfer of the effects of training is sought it must be looked for in the greater relative improvement of the practised group. That is, if there has been any transfer the practised group must show a greater improvement than the unpractised.

Note on the Method of Mean Error.—The method employed in this experiment to produce a line equal to a given standard line is that known as the method of mean error. The variables produced by the subject are averaged and the mean result is, as it were, what the person has in mind. But the individual variables naturally differ from each other as he does not always hit his own mark. The differences between the mean and the individual variables, calculated without regard to algebraic sign, may be regarded as the person's error of production at each attempt. If, therefore, we calculate the mean variation of the variables we arrive at the 'mean variable error.' The lower this quantity the more consistent is the person with his own idea of the standard. By finding the coefficient of variability, i.e. the ratio of this error to the mean, a relative measure of consistency is obtained by which different persons may be compared.

Measures of accuracy of estimation may be derived from the 'crude constant error' or the 'crude average error.' The former is the difference between the mean of the variables and the standard length; the latter is the mean of the deviations of the individual variables from the standard, regardless of sign. These measures, as their names imply, are rough and unanalysed, but for the purposes of our experiment further analysis is quite unnecessary. For we are not concerned with the various factors, such as spatial errors due to the relative position of the standard and variable lines, as these do not affect our problem.

The method of treating these factors and other refinements may be studied in Titchener's *Experimental Psychology*, Vol. II., Part I., pp. 70 foll., or Myers' *Text-book of Experimental Psychology*, 2nd ed., pp. 190 foll.

For a full discussion of the present type of experiment see the author's *Educational Psychology*, Ch. VII.

CHAPTER IX

MENTAL FATIGUE

Experiment 28

The purpose of this experiment is to investigate the nature of mental fatigue.

The material to be used is that employed in Experiment 5 on the attainment curve, namely continuous texts (see Appendix II.).

The method of procedure and scoring is exactly the same as in the above experiment. If the same set of subjects take part in both experiments it may be necessary to provide extra sheets of continuous texts. The experiment consists of two parts. The subjects to be experimented upon are given 4 five-minute tests in the morning when they are fresh. On the basis of the total marks gained in these tests, they are divided into two equivalent groups, A and B. If it is feasible these tests should be given on different days; otherwise on the same day with an interval between them to prevent fatigue.

Group A assemble about a week later and are given a further 5 minute test (Test *a*) in the morning, whilst Group B work the same test in the evening after a day's work. The following morning Group B are given a 5 minute test (Test *b*) and Group A work the same test in the evening. An attempt should be made to give these tests on days when the subjects have a heavy day's work.

The number of marks gained per minute (or preferably in each half minute) is found for the individual subjects. Then the mean variation and the coefficient of variability are calculated for each subject.

The following table is drawn up in order to compare the results:

Date	*Time*		*Average Mark per Minute (or ½ Minute)*	*Average Coefficient of Variability*
	a.m. }	Test *a* { Group A		
	p.m. }	" B		
	a.m. }	Test *b* { " B		
	p.m. }	" A		

The effects of fatigue should be sought in the last column, i.e. in the greater variability of the evening groups. It would make an instructive research experiment to compare men and women with respect to fatiguability by this test.

A full discussion of results will be found in the author's *Educational Psychology*, Ch. XII.

PART II

STATISTICAL

CHAPTER X

ASSOCIATION

Measures of Relationship

In psychological investigations we have frequently to determine whether certain capacities, qualities, or attributes are related to each other or whether they are independent. Thus, we may require to know whether intelligence varies concomitantly with sensory acuity or whether the variations of each capacity are unrelated to one another. We shall consider four statistical methods by which the concomitance of the variables may be tested, each being employed for some special set of data.

When two capacities are not quantitatively graded, but their presence or absence merely noted, we use the *coefficient of association* to determine the degree of their interdependence. By this method we may divide parents and children, for instance, into such classes as sane or insane, and determine from the relative proportions of each whether insanity in the parents is associated with the same attribute in the children. In this way some light may be shed on the question of heredity.

Suppose, again, we have divided persons into those with good and bad vision. It may now be possible to take each class separately and further subdivide it into different minor classes. Thus, the bad vision class might be subdivided into classes with myopia and astigmatism. It is not necessary for the division into classes to be dichotomous, as in the case of association, but any number of subdivisions may be made in each class. When it is possible to make such a qualitative classification we may use the *contingency coefficient* as the measure of relationship between two characters.

If a *quantitative* classification is possible, as when the attributes or characters can be specified in terms of numerical units, two other measures of inter-relationship are employed. Thus, both intelligence and scholastic attainments can be determined by means of standard tests, by which means numerical values can be assigned to them. In such cases the degree of relationship of the two variables may be measured by the *correlation ratio* or the *correlation coefficient*. The former of these two can be used in all cases, but the latter is confined to those cases in which the concomitant variation approximates to a linear form; a restriction which will be explained later.

For the sake of convenience, the calculation of all the above four measures is so arranged that the maximum degree of relationship is denoted by unity, and complete independence of the variables by zero. The degree of relationship is, therefore, measured by a fraction lying between zero and unity.

The meaning of the four measures of relationship will become clearer when the methods of calculation are understood.

Association

Let the capital letters A, B, C, etc., be used to denote attributes or qualities or capacities; the same letter with a bar, $\bar{A}$, $\bar{B}$, $\bar{C}$, etc., to denote the absence of attributes or capacities. Thus if A denotes the power to use visual imagery, $\bar{A}$ asserts the absence of such power.

Juxtaposition of letters will be taken to imply combination of attributes; thus if B denotes intelligence and C visual acuity, BC implies intelligence and visual acuity in the same person, and $B\bar{C}$ an intelligent but not visually acute person.

The series of observations to which any inquiry is restricted is called the *universe of discourse* or the *group*. If such a group is divided into classes, determined by the presence or absence of attributes, the number of individuals in any given class is called the *frequency*, which may be denoted by placing brackets round the attribute or attributes. Thus if A denotes auditory acuity and B visual acuity, (A) is the number or frequency of the class A, (AB) the number of the class AB, i.e. the number of those who are both visually and aurally acute; $(\bar{A}B)$ the number of those who are visually acute, but not aurally acute; and so on. N is used as the number denoting the frequency of the universe or whole group.

With n attributes we must clearly get 2^n classes, if each class is specified by n positive or negative attributes. Thus for two attributes A and B we get the following class-frequencies (AB), $(A\bar{B})$, $(\bar{A}B)$, $(\bar{A}\bar{B})$.

If there is no relationship of any kind between the attributes A and B in a given group we should expect to find the same proportion of A's among the B's as amongst the $\bar{B}$'s. Thus, if intelligence and sensory acuity are independent of each other we ought to find the same proportion of intelligent people amongst those who have acute senses as amongst those who have not, in a sufficiently large group.

This *criterion of independence* may be expressed, in the terminology here used, as follows:

$$\frac{(AB)}{(B)} = \frac{(A\bar{B})}{(\bar{B})} \qquad \text{(1)}$$

or:

$$\frac{(AB)}{(A)} = \frac{(\bar{A}B)}{(\bar{A})} \qquad \text{(2)}$$

The former of these expressions would read: The proportion of A's amongst the B's, is the same as that amongst the non-B's. The latter expression similarly expresses the equality of the proportion of B's amongst the A's and non-A's.

If the left-hand side in either of the above equations

is greater or less than the right, A and B are said to be *positively* or *negatively associated.*

The criterion of independence may also be stated thus; the proportion of A's among the B's is the same as the proportion of A's in the whole universe or group.

i.e. $$\frac{(AB)}{(B)} = \frac{(A)}{N}$$

or $$(AB) = \frac{(A).(B)}{N} \quad \ldots\ldots\ldots\ldots\ldots (3)$$

If, therefore, $$(AB) \gtrless \frac{(A).(B)}{N}$$

A and B will be positively or negatively associated.

It is also clear that, if A and B are independent, relations similar to (3) must be found amongst the other classes in the group, thus:

$$(A\bar{B}) = \frac{(A).(\bar{B})}{N}$$

$$(\bar{A}B) = \frac{(\bar{A}).(B)}{N}$$

$$(\bar{A}\bar{B}) = \frac{(\bar{A}).(\bar{B})}{N}$$

For the naming of any class as positive or negative is entirely arbitrary; the same class, for instance, may be described as sane or not-insane.

From the above equalities it follows at once that

$$(AB)\,(\bar{A}\bar{B})=(A\bar{B})(\bar{A}B) \qquad \ldots\ldots (4)$$

This equation may be regarded as another form of the criterion of independence.

For complete association of A and B, either or both of the frequencies $(A\bar{B})$, $(\bar{A}B)$ must be zero; for complete dissociation (negative association) either or both (AB), $(\bar{A}\bar{B})$ must be zero.

The following equation, therefore, may be used to measure the intensity of association between A and B:

$$Q=\frac{(AB)\,(\bar{A}\bar{B})-(A\bar{B})\,(\bar{A}B)}{(AB)\,(\bar{A}\bar{B})+(A\bar{B})\,(\bar{A}B)}$$

$Q=0$ when the attributes are independent, for then the numerator is zero by equation (4). $Q=1$ for complete association, for then the second term in both numerator and denominator is zero, by the preceding paragraph. $Q=-1$ for complete dissociation, for then the first term in numerator and denominator is zero. Q is therefore called the *coefficient of association.* Values from 0 to 1, or 0 to -1 measure degrees of association and dissociation respectively.

Another form for measuring the intensity of association is called the coefficient of colligation (ω), and its formula is identical with the above except for the square-root signs.

$$\omega=\frac{\sqrt{(AB)\,(\bar{A}\bar{B})}-\sqrt{(A\bar{B})\,(\bar{A}B)}}{\sqrt{(AB)\,(\bar{A}\bar{B})}+\sqrt{(A\bar{B})\,(\bar{A}B)}}$$

ω gives smaller values than Q; and for purposes of comparison with coefficients of correlation it is a better measure to use.

Example.—The following table is from the "Inheritance of the Insane Diathesis" (*Francis Galton Laboratory Memoirs*, ii., 1907).

PARENTS

	Insane A	*Not Insane $\bar{A}$*	*Totals*
Children: Insane *B*	49=(AB)	361=($\bar{A}$B)	410=(B)
Not insane *$\bar{B}$*	149=(A$\bar{B}$)	40,441=($\bar{A}\bar{B}$)	40,590=($\bar{B}$)
Totals	198=(A)	40,802=($\bar{A}$)	41,000=N

It is required to find whether insanity in the parents is associated with insanity in the offspring.

We make use of equations (1) and (2).

Proportion of insane children among insane parents

$$\frac{(AB)}{(A)} = \frac{49}{198} = 25 \text{ per cent.}$$

Proportion of insane children among sane parents

$$\frac{(\bar{A}B)}{(\bar{A})} = \frac{361}{40802} = \cdot 9 \text{ per cent.}$$

Or we may start from the parents:

Proportion of insane parents of insane children

$$\frac{(AB)}{(B)} = \frac{49}{410} = 12 \text{ per cent.}$$

Proportion of insane parents of sane children

$$\frac{(A\bar{B})}{(\bar{B})} = \frac{149}{40590} = \cdot 4 \text{ per cent.}$$

Either comparison shows a strong association.

To find the degree of association, we get:

$$Q = \frac{49 \times 40441 - 149 \times 361}{49 \times 40441 + 149 \times 361} = \cdot 95. \quad (\omega = \cdot 72)$$

Exercise.—Construct the complete table, as in the example above, from the following data and find (1) whether there is any association, (2) the coefficient of association, (3) coefficient of colligation.

Let A denote insane parent, $\bar{A}$ sane parent.

Let B denote insane offspring, $\bar{B}$ sane offspring.

$(AB) = 52$, $(A\bar{B}) = 158$, $(\bar{A}B) = 360$, $(\bar{A}\bar{B}) = 20030$.

(Answer: $Q = \cdot 90$; $\omega = \cdot 62$.)

CHAPTER XI

CONTINGENCY

All the remaining measures of relationship presuppose a thorough grasp of the following schema. Letters and brackets are interpreted as before.

	A_1	A_2	....	....	....	A_p	....			*Total*
B_1	(A_1B_1)	(A_2B_1)				(A_pB_1)				(B_1)
B_2	(A_1B_2)	(A_2B_2)				(A_pB_2)				(B_2)
....										
....										
B_s	(A_1B_s)	(A_2B_s)				(A_pB_s)				(B_s)
....										
Total	(A_1)	(A_2)				(A_p)				N

So far we have considered only a twofold or dichotomous classification, the A's being divided into B's and $\bar{B}$'s. But we may classify the A's themselves into different classes, A_1, A_2, etc., and each class into an '*array*' of B classes. We get, in this way, a number of sub-classes or '*cells*,' forming what is called a *contingency table*, as above, where the frequency (A_pB_s) denotes the number of individuals having both the characters or attributes

A_p and B_s; and so on for each cell. The frequencies shown at the end of the rows, e.g. (B_s) or at the base of the columns, e.g. (A_p), are the totals of different arrays; and the total number of all the frequencies, or the number of observations in the universe of discourse is N. It is, of course, merely a matter of convenience whether the A or B arrays are placed horizontally or vertically.

Now if B is *independent* of A, it clearly follows that the frequency distribution of the array of B's is the same in every column of A's. In other words the proportional distribution of frequencies in the cells of any column is the same as that in the cells of the whole group, which is shown in the column of totals.

Expressed symbolically, we may state that A and B are *completely independent* if the following relation holds good for every cell in the contingency table.

$$\frac{(A_p\ B_s)}{(A_p)} = \frac{(B_s)}{N}$$

Or, if we denote the *independence frequency* of the cell $A_p\ B_s$ by $(A_p\ B_s)_o$, we get

$$(A_p\ B_s)_o = \frac{(A_p)\ (B_s)}{N}$$

If the cell has any other frequency than this, B is *not* independent of A, but is somehow *contingent* on it.

The deviation of the actual frequency of any cell from its independence frequency, i.e.

$$d_{ps} = (A_p\ B_s) - (A_p\ B_s)_o$$

is called the contingency of the cell; and a measure of contingency must be, in some way, dependent on the values of d for the whole table. But the values of d may be positive or negative, and, as either is equally significant, we take the square of the deviations so as to eliminate the negative signs. Also, our measure of contingency must be relative both to the independence frequencies and to the total number of observations in the group.

Hence the *mean square contingency* of the cell

$$A_pB_s \text{ is } \frac{d^2_{ps}}{(A_pB_s)_o \times N}$$

For the whole table the mean square contingency S is:

$$S = \Sigma \left[\frac{d^2_{ps}}{(A_pB_s)_o \times N} \right].$$

Now the sum of a number of squares can only vanish if each is zero. If, therefore, S=0 each cell must have its independence frequency; i.e. $d_{ps}=0$. In such a case the characters are independent.

We can construct a coefficient of contingency, called the *mean square contingency coefficient,* thus:

$$C = \sqrt{\frac{S}{1+S}}.$$

This coefficient is zero if S=0, i.e. if the characters A and B are completely independent. If S is not zero C approaches towards unity as S increases. It only reaches unity for an infinite number of cells, but for 4×4 cells its value is about ·87 and for 5×5 the value approximates to ·9. Thus the coefficient should normally be used for a 5×5 fold table or any finer classification. We have thus arrived at a measure of the concomitant variation of A and B.

Example.—The following contingency table is from "Inheritance of Vision," *Galton Eugenics Laboratory Memoirs*, V. (1909):

REFRACTION CLASS AND AGE (BOYS)

Refraction Class	*Age*					*Totals*
	5–7	7–9	9–11	11–13	13–15	
Normal	54	112	134	114	41	455
Hypermetropia	19	24	27	26	7	103
Hypermetropic astigmatism	12	19	10	13	10	64
Mixed astigmatism ..	4	6	4	4	1	19
Myopia and myopic astigmatism	0	5	5	4	4	18
Total	89	166	180	161	63	659

Required to find the mean square contingency coefficient for this 5×5 fold table.

First we find the independence value of the frequency of each cell by the formula

$$(A_pB_s)_o = \frac{(A_p)\,(B_s)}{N}.$$

INDEPENDENCE VALUES

	Ages				
	4–7	7–9	9–11	11–13	13–15
Normal	61·4	114·7	124·5	111	43·5
Hypermetropia	13·9	26·0	28·2	25·2	9·85
Hypermetropic astigmatism	8·65	16·1	17·5	15·6	6·12
Mixed astigmatism	2·57	4·78	5·20	4·65	1·82
Myopia, etc.	2·43	4·55	4·92	4·40	1·72

From the above two tables, by simple subtraction for each cell, we get the values of the deviations.

$$d_{ps} = (A_p B_s) - (A_p B_s)_o$$

VALUES OF d_{ps}

7·40	2·70	9·50	3·0	2·50
5·10	2·0	1·20	0·80	2·85
3·35	2·90	7·50	2·60	3·88
1·43	1·22	1·20	0·65	0·82
2·43	0·45	0·08	0·40	2·28

Thence we derive the values of $\dfrac{d^2_{ps}}{(A_p B_s)_o}$ for each cell,

0·890	0·064	0·730	0·081	0·144
1·880	0·152	0·051	0·026	0·827
1·300	0·520	3·220	0·435	2·460
0·800	0·312	0·270	0·091	0·370
2·430	0·045	0·001	0·036	3·250

By adding up all the cells in this table we get

$$\Sigma \left[\frac{d^2_{ps}}{(A_p B_s)_o}\right] = 20{\cdot}385$$

Dividing by N (=659) gives the value of S.
Whence C=·17.

Exercise.—Find the mean square contingency coefficient of refraction class and age from the following table.

REFRACTION CLASS AND AGE (GIRLS)

Refraction Class	*Age*					*Total*
	5–7	7–9	9–11	11–13	13–15	
Normal	56	83	107	76	29	351
Hypermetropia	15	23	28	12	6	84
Hypermetropic astigmatism	24	21	10	15	6	76
Mixed astigmatism	10	4	4	3	1	22
Myopia and myopic astigmatism	0	4	2	11	3	20
Total	105	135	151	117	45	553

(Answer: C=·28)

CHAPTER XII

FREQUENCY DIAGRAMS

Frequency Distribution

The following table shows the marks gained by 140 students in some tests on reasoning. The marks are called variables and the number of students attaining to each interval of marks is the frequency.

Variables	0	$\frac{1}{2}$–1	$1\frac{1}{2}$–2	$2\frac{1}{2}$–3	$3\frac{1}{2}$–4	$4\frac{1}{2}$–5	$5\frac{1}{2}$–6
Frequency	2	11	36	40	31	14	6

Such a table is called a *frequency distribution*. In order to represent the distribution graphically a column proportional in height to the frequency is placed over each class-interval or variable, and the resulting figure is known as a *histogram*. Any portion of the area of the histogram represents the number of individuals who are found within the corresponding class-intervals. If the class-intervals are continually reduced in size whilst the number of variables is proportionately increased the histogram ultimately becomes a smooth *frequency-curve*. In such a curve the area between any two ordinates is proportional to the number of observations falling within those limits.

The Normal Curve

An important type of frequency curve is that known as the 'normal' curve; and familiarity with its form and properties is essential to students of practical psychology. The following considerations will aid in elucidating this

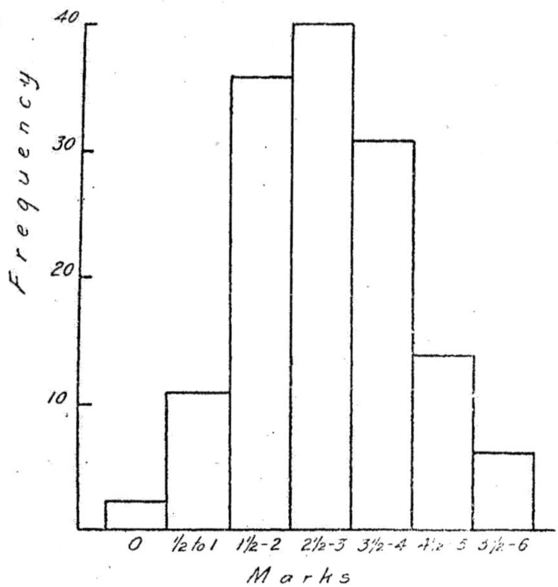

FIG. 12.—HISTOGRAM FOR REASONING ABILITY (140 SUBJECTS)

type of curve. Let us consider a set of variables, such as the heights of men of a particular nation. It is clear that these variables are subject to an indefinitely large number of independent causes of variation. We may regard the mean height as a quantity determined by the hereditary relationship of the individuals; whilst there are a large multitude of independent causes producing deviations from the mean. Suppose that all the men inherit the same height, but that there are (say) four independent causes at work, each of which is capable of increasing the height by one inch; so that none, or one, or more of these causes may affect the height of any individual. From these data it is evident that deviations from the inherited height can be calculated by the theory of combinations. Thus, no deviation will occur in one way, a deviation of 1 inch in four ways, i.e. ${}_4C_1$, a deviation of 2 inches in six ways, i.e. ${}_4C_2$, and so on. Hence we get the table:

Deviations	0	1	2	3	4 inches.
Frequency	1	4	6	4	1

From this table we can calculate the mean deviation, namely 2 inches.

If the causes producing the deviations from the mean act two in the negative direction and two in the positive, it is evident that each deviation will, in the long run, be diminished by 2 inches; but the frequencies will be unaltered. We should then get:

Deviations	−2	−1	0	1	2
Frequency	1	4	6	4	1

This table really represents the frequency-distribution which results from two positive and two negative independent causes of deviation of equal magnitude.

Similarly, if there are 5 independent causes producing positive deviations from the mean and 5 producing negative deviations, we get:

Deviations	−5	−4	−3	−2	−1	0	1	2	3	4	5
Frequency	1	10	45	120	210	252	210	120	45	10	1

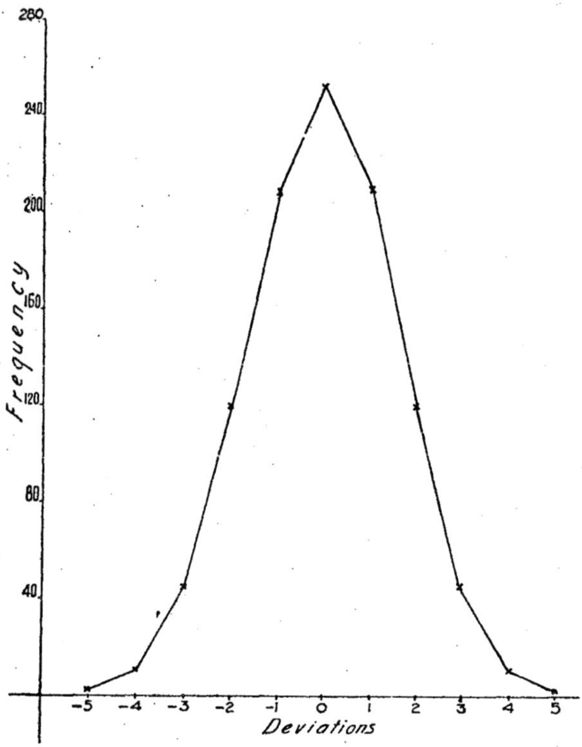

FIG. 13.—FREQUENCY DISTRIBUTION OF 10 INDEPENDENT VARIABLES, 5 POSITIVE AND 5 NEGATIVE

It will be seen that the frequencies are the coefficients obtained by expanding the binomial $(1+1)^{10}$.

The resulting frequency distribution is shown in the accompanying figure.

By parity of reasoning we may imagine the number of independent causes increased indefinitely and at the same time the amount of deviation produced by each may be supposed indefinitely diminished. In this way we should arrive at a continuous curve, called the normal frequency curve or the curve of error. The equation to this curve is

$$y_x = y_o e^{-\frac{x^2}{2\sigma^2}}$$

where e is the base of the Napierian logarithms, x the deviation from the mean, y_x the frequency of x, y_o the frequency of the mean value, and σ the standard deviation of the distribution. The term standard deviation is explained in a later section.

Thus the normal curve is completely defined when we have assigned the origin of x and know the values of y_o and σ. The area of this curve, or of any portion of it cut off by two ordinates, represents the number of observations within those limits. It is obvious that any alteration in y_o produces a proportionate alteration in the area. Again any alteration in σ produces a proportionate alteration in the area, for the values of y_x are the same for the same values of $\frac{x}{\sigma}$ and therefore doubling σ doubles the distance of every ordinate from the mean, and consequently doubles the area. In drawing the normal curve it must be remembered that, since the equation involves $\frac{x}{\sigma}$ *deviations are all to be measured in terms of* σ.

The value of y_0 may be determined once for all, and the complete equation written thus,

$$y = \frac{N}{\sigma\sqrt{2\pi}} e^{-\frac{x^2}{2\sigma^2}}$$

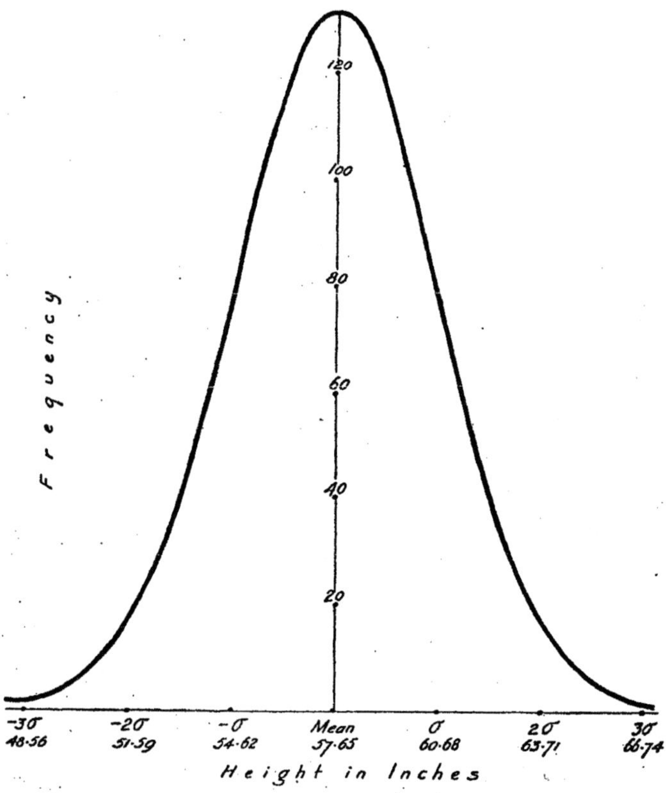

FIG. 14.—A NORMAL CURVE: DISTRIBUTION OF THE HEIGHTS OF AUSTRALIAN GIRLS OF 13 YEARS OF AGE

Since this involves quantities which are the same for all curves of this kind, the values of the ordinates as fractional parts of the mean ordinate are recorded in tables (see p. 122) for all values of $\frac{x}{\sigma}$, and the curve is constructed from such tables.

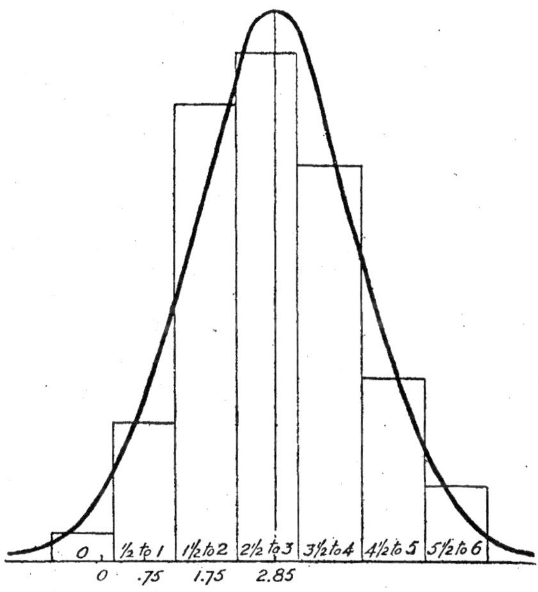

FIG. 15.—NORMAL CURVE OF REASONING ABILITY: THE CURVE OF CLOSEST FIT TO THE DATA OF THE HISTOGRAM

The curve on p. 120 is an example of such a normal curve.

The figure on this page shows the relation of the histogram (previously considered) to the normal curve. The latter is the curve of 'closest fit' to the data from which the histogram was drawn. As the area of the curve is roughly equal to that of the histogram it would suggest that reasoning ability is 'normally' distributed.

The following tables show the values of the ordinates at different distances $\frac{x}{\sigma}$ from the mean $(\frac{x}{\sigma}=0)$ and also the area of any portion of the normal curve.

ORDINATES OF NORMAL CURVE

$\frac{x}{\sigma}$	y	$\frac{x}{\sigma}$	y
0	1·000	1·8	·198
0·2	·980	2·0	·135
0·4	·923	2·2	·089
0·6	·835	2·4	·056
0·8	·726	2·6	·034
1·0	·606	2·8	·020
1·2	·487	3·0	·011
1·4	·375	3·2	·006
1·6	·278	3·4	·003
		3·6	·001

FRACTION OF THE AREA TO THE LEFT OF THE ORDINATE AT ABSCISSA $\frac{x}{\sigma}$

$\frac{x}{\sigma}$	*Fraction of Area*	$\frac{x}{\sigma}$	*Fraction of Area*
0	·500	1·8	·964
0·2	·579	2·0	·977
0·4	·655	2·2	·986
0·6	·726	2·4	·992
0·8	·788	2·6	·995
1·0	·841	2·8	·997
1·2	·885	3·0	·999
1·4	·919	3·2	·9993
1·6	·945	3·4	·9997

Exercise (1).—Find by the use of the tables the fraction of the area of the normal curve included between the ordinates of abscissæ $\pm \cdot 675\sigma$.

(Answer: ·5 approximately)

Exercise (2).—(*a*) On the same axes and with the same mean value draw two normal curves one having double the standard deviation of the other.

(*b*) Draw two normal curves in one of which the value of y_0 is half that in the other, the mean and standard deviation being the same.

Exercise (3).—The mean of 1,000 observations, normally distributed, is 40 inches and the standard deviation (σ) is 3 inches. Draw the normal curve and find, by the tables, the number of observations below 32 inches and above 45 inches.

(Answer: 4, 48)

CHAPTER XIII

AVERAGES

In any frequency-distribution there are two important quantities to be considered, (*a*) the value of the variable round which the observations are centred, (*b*) the range or dispersion of the variables. Measures of the former quantity are called *averages*, of the latter *deviations*.

The Mean

The two most frequently used averages in psychology are the mean (M) and the median (Mi). If X denotes the value of any variable, f the frequency of its occurrence, and n the total number of observations, then

$$M = \frac{1}{n} \Sigma (f. X)$$

The table below illustrates a labour-saving method of calculating the mean of a frequency-distribution when the number of observations is large. The first column shows the heights of boys of 13 years, in inches. An arbitrary variable A (=56 inches) has been chosen and the deviations (δ) from this are shown in the third column. The fourth column shows the total deviations from the chosen variable. The fifth column is obtained by multiplying the fourth by the third. It will be used later, and can be ignored at present.

The mean is obtained by finding the mean of the deviations and adding the arbitrary variable.

FREQUENCY DISTRIBUTION OF THE HEIGHTS OF AUSTRALIAN BOYS OF 13 YEARS

Heights (Inches)	*Frequency* f	*Deviations from A* δ	$f.\delta$	$f.\delta^2$
47	1	−9	− 9	81
48	3	−8	− 24	192
49	2	−7	− 14	98
50	5	−6	− 30	180
51	17	−5	− 85	425
52	31	−4	− 124	496
53	56	−3	− 168	504
54	107	−2	− 214	428
55	120	−1	− 120	120
			− 788	
A=56	163	0		
57	136	1	136	136
58	108	2	216	432
59	87	3	261	783
60	67	4	268	1072
61	49	5	245	1225
62	23	6	138	828
63	11	7	77	539
64	7	8	56	448
65	3	9	27	243
66	1	10	10 + 1434	100

$n = 997$ $\Sigma(f \cdot \delta) = 646$

$$M = 56 + \frac{646}{997} = 56{\cdot}65 \text{ inches.}$$

$\Sigma(f.\delta^2) = 8330$

$$s^2 = \frac{8330}{997} = 8{\cdot}36$$

$$\therefore \sigma^2 = 8{\cdot}36 - ({\cdot}65)^2$$
$$= 7{\cdot}94$$

The above method may be generalised thus: Let A be any arbitrary variable, X any other variable, and let δ be the deviation of X from A; i.e.

$$X = A + \delta.$$

Then $$\Sigma (f.X) = \Sigma (f.A) + \Sigma (f.\delta)$$

$\therefore$ $$\frac{\Sigma (f.X)}{n} = \frac{\Sigma (f.A)}{n} + \frac{\Sigma (f.\delta)}{n}$$

But A is a constant.

$\therefore$ $$M = A + \frac{1}{n} \Sigma (f.\delta)$$

or $$\Sigma(f.\delta) = n(M - A)$$

This equation is of fundamental importance in the theory of correlation. It may be expressed in words thus: The sum total of the deviations of n variables from any origin A is n times the deviation of the mean from the same origin.

If we select M as the origin from which to measure the deviations, the equation becomes

$$\Sigma(f.\delta) = (M - M) = 0$$

Thus the sum of deviations of the variables from the mean is zero.

The Median

The median (M*i*) is defined either as (*a*) the central value of the variable when the values are arranged in order of magnitude, or as (*b*) the value of the variable such that greater and smaller values occur with equal frequency. It is obvious that, in a frequency-curve, the vertical line through the median divides the area of the curve into two equal parts. Two other variables may be found, the verticals through which cut off a quarter and three-quarters respectively of the total area of the curve; these are called the lower and upper *quartiles*, Q_1 and Q_3.

The values of the variables which divide the frequency into ten equal parts are called *deciles;* the fifth decile being, of course, the median. Similarly, the value P of the variable below which there is p per cent. of the total frequency and therefore 100-p per cent. above, is called a *percentile.*

The calculation of the median and quartiles may be understood from the following example. Suppose a test is given to seventeen candidates, and the marks, arranged in order of magnitude, are:

9 11 11·5 12·5 13 13·5 13·5 14 14·5 15 15 15 16 17 17 18 19·5

$Q_1 = 12·75$ Mi $Q_3 = 16·5$

The median 14·5 is found by counting up to the 9th variable, for this is the variable above and below which there are an equal number of readings. The lower quartile should have (by definition) $\frac{17}{4} = 4\frac{1}{4}$ readings below it and the upper quartile $4\frac{1}{4}$ readings above it. As this is impossible, we select an arbitrary point, namely, the mean between the 4th and 5th readings for Q_1 and the mean between the 13th and 14th readings for Q_3. But another method is to take the 5th reading from the bottom, namely, 13; and the 5th from the top, namely, 16 for the quartiles. This is equally arbitrary, and assumes that the 5th readings from each end are divided by the quartiles so as to fall partly below and partly above them.

The median is a suitable average to use when there are abnormally large or small readings in a series of variables. Thus in the above series, if the final reading had been 36·5 instead of 19·5, the average would be increased by unity, but the median would be unchanged.

The median, quartiles, and the other percentiles may be determined by a graphical method. Consider the frequency distribution of the table on p. 125.

Heights	47	48	49	50	51	52	53	54	55	56
Frequency	1	3	2	5	17	31	56	107	120	163
Integrated frequency	1	4	6	11	28	59	115	222	342	505

Heights	57	58	59	60	61	62	63	64	65	66
Frequency	136	108	87	67	49	23	11	7	3	1
Integrated frequency	641	749	836	903	952	975	986	993	996	997

The frequencies are added up step by step to give the integrated frequencies. The latter are then plotted against the heights as shown in the diagram. The base line is next divided into 100 equal *grades*, and the ordinates at each grade are the percentiles. Such a curve is called by Galton an *ogive* curve. From it we may read off at once the percentage of individuals above and below any given height. This method of plotting enables us to compare two statistical groups by finding the centesimal grade in one group, which corresponds to the median in the other group.

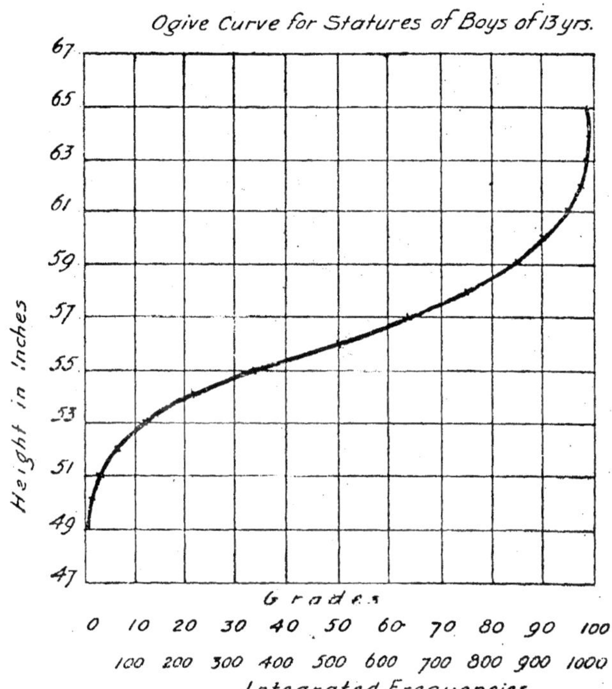

FIG. 16.

Exercise.—The table shows the I.Q. of 170 children of 8 to 10 years. Draw the ogive curve and find the median.

I.Q.	65–69	70–74	75–79	80–84	85–89	90–94	95–99
No.	2	4	4	9	11	21	21

I.Q.	100–4	105–9	110–14	115–19	120–24	125–29	130
No.	36	21	18	14	5	3	1

CHAPTER XIV

DEVIATIONS

The simplest measure of dispersion of a series of variables is the *quartile deviation* (Q), sometimes called the semi-interquartile range. It is found thus:

$$Q=\frac{Q_3-Q_1}{2}$$

In our illustration on p. 127

$$Q=\frac{16{\cdot}5-12{\cdot}75}{2}=1{\cdot}87$$

Another measure is the *mean deviation* (m.d.), sometimes known as the mean variation (m.v.). It is found by calculating the arithmetic mean of the deviations from some average, without regard to sign.

Variable X	*Deviations from Mean* x	*Deviations from Median* x_1
26	+3	+4
24	+1	+2
21	−2	−1
22	−1	0
19	−4	−3
20	−3	−2
29	+6	+7
161	20	19
M = 23 Mi = 22	*m.d.* = 2·8[illegible]	2·71

The second column shows the calculation of m.d. from the mean, the third from the median. Deviations can be measured from any other value; but it may be proved that m.d. is least when deviations are measured from the median.

The most widely used measure of dispersion is called the *standard deviation*, and its calculation is shown below.

Variables X	*Deviations from A* δ	δ^2	*Deviations from Mean* x	x^2
12	−5	25	−7	49
13	−4	16	−6	36
14	−3	9	−5	25
A= 17	0	0	−2	4
18	+1	1	−1	1
19	2	4	0	0
21	4	16	+2	4
22	5	25	3	9
25	8	64	6	36
29	12	144	10	100
190		304		264
M= 19		$s^2=30{\cdot}4$		$\sigma^2=26{\cdot}4$
		$s = 5{\cdot}51$		$\sigma = 5{\cdot}14$

The table on p. 125 shows the short method of calculation when there is a large number of variables.

In the above series of readings we have chosen an arbitrary variable (A) as the origin. Then the root-mean-square deviation (s) from this origin is given by the formula

$$s=\sqrt{\frac{\Sigma\,(\delta^2)}{N}}$$

In this expression δ is the deviation of each variable from the origin and N is the number of variables.

The standard deviation σ is the *root-mean-squa, e deviation from the mean,* i.e.:

$$\sigma = \sqrt{\frac{\Sigma (x^2)}{N}}$$

If the number of variables is small, it is better to use the expression:

$$\sigma = \sqrt{\frac{\Sigma (x^2)}{N - 1}}$$

If d is the deviation of the arbitrary origin from the mean (in our example $d = 19 - 17 = 2$), then it may easily be shown that

$$\sigma^2 = s^2 - d^2$$

The standard deviation is, therefore, the least possible root-mean-square deviation. It saves arithmetic (as above) to calculate deviations from some arbitrary origin and then to deduce the standard deviation from the last formula.

Thus, in our example,

$$\sigma^2 = 30{\cdot}4 - 4 = 26{\cdot}4$$

The following equation should be carefully noted:

$$N\sigma^2 = \Sigma (x^2)$$

where x is the deviation of each variable from the mean.

Probable Error

In the section describing the normal curve it was pointed out that such a distribution is the result of one or more predominating factors associated with a very large number of small factors operating independently of each other. Now in the attempt to measure any quantity, the errors of observation, which may be regarded as compounded of a large number of independent causes, will be distributed in accordance with the normal curve of frequency. Consequently this curve is often called the 'curve of errors.'

We have also seen that, in such a curve, the ordinates through the quartiles enclose half the area of the curve, i.e. half the number of observations is included within these lines, and half lie outside these limits. Hence, there is an even chance that any observation will be found within or without these limits. If the distribution of errors is 'normal' the *probable error* (P.E.) is the quantity such that we may expect greater and less errors to occur with equal frequency. Neither of the terms 'probable' nor 'error' is a happy one. It is better to define P.E. as that deviation above and below the mean which together include half of the total frequency. In other words, half the number of variables fall *outside* ±P.E. An approximate value of P.E. is given by the quartile deviation.

A more exact value is $\cdot 6745\sigma$, i.e:

$$\text{P.E.} = \cdot 6745 \sqrt{\frac{\Sigma (x^2)}{\text{N}}}$$

If the number of variables is small it is better to use the formula

$$\text{P.E.} = \cdot 6745 \sqrt{\frac{\Sigma (x^2)}{\text{N} - 1}}$$

Note.—In calculating measures of relationship it must be borne in mind that no coefficient is 'significant' unless it is at least four times its probable error.

Relative Dispersion

So far we have considered absolute deviations, but, for purposes of comparison, it is sometimes desirable to calculate relative values. Thus, if we were comparing the deviations of the heights of men and women, it would be obviously necessary to refer such deviations to the corresponding average heights in order to discover which are the more variable. For such relative purposes one of the following *coefficients of variation* is used

(1) $\frac{\text{m.d.}}{\text{M}} \times 100.$

(2) $\frac{\text{Q}}{\text{M}i} \times 100.$

(3) $\frac{\sigma}{\text{M}} \times 100$ (Pearson's)

Equivalent Groups.—It is often necessary to divide a single group of persons into two equivalent groups, with reference to some capacity or character. Suppose, for example, that by means of tests of memory, a group of subjects is arranged in the following numerical order of merit:

$$a_1, a_2, a_3, a_4, a_5, a_6, a_7, a_8, \text{etc.}$$

To get equivalent groups they are arranged thus:

Group 1	*Group* 2
a_1	a_2
a_4	a_3
a_5	a_6
a_8	a_7
a_9	a_{10}
a_{12}	a_{11}
a_{13}	a_{14}

In order that the groups may be treated as equivalent, the coefficients of variation should be approximately the same. Unless this condition is satisfied the grouping is unsatisfactory for comparative purposes.

Exercise 1.—The following table shows the frequency-distribution of the heights, in inches, of 994 girls of 13 years of age.

Heights ..	47	48	49	50	51	52	53	54	55	56
Frequency ..	4	1	5	5	12	15	42	62	91	98

Heights ..	57	58	59	60	61	62	63	64	65	66
Frequency ..	116	146	121	102	79	50	27	12	4	2

Find the mean, the median, mean deviation, standard deviation, probable error, coefficient of variation. By comparison with the table on p. 125, find whether boys or girls are more variable in height.

Answer: M=57·56, Mi=57·31, σ=3·05.

Exercise 2.—Fit a normal curve to the above frequency-distribution.

First find

$$y_o = \frac{N}{\sigma\sqrt{2\pi}} = \frac{994}{3{\cdot}05\sqrt{2\pi}}$$

Take the mean (57·56) as the origin and mark off a scale showing fractions of the standard deviation (3·03) up to ±3σ. At these points erect the ordinates given in the table on p. 122, multiplying each by y_o.

Exercise 3.—(*a*) Construct the ogive curve for the given frequency distribution, and find from it the quartile deviation. (*b*) Hence find an approximate value for the standard deviation. (*c*) Find what centesimal grade in the group of girls corresponds to the median grade of the boys' group.

CHAPTER XV

CORRELATION RATIO

The contingency table printed below was obtained by giving Binet-Simon tests and scholastic tests to 427 children in London schools.

		Mental Ratio A					*Total*	
		A_1	A_2	A_3	A_4	A_5		
		85 –	90 –	95 –	100 –	105 –		
Educational ratio B	B_1 85 –	13	16	7	2	1	39	(B_1)
	B_2 90 –	12	22	15	19	5	73	(B_2)
	B_3 95 –	10	28	41	35	23	137	(B_3)
	B_4 100 –	4	17	35	44	27	127	(B_4)
	B_5 105 –	1	5	9	15	21	51	(B_5)
Total		40	88	107	115	77	427	=N
		(A_1)	(A_2)	(A_3)	(A_4)	(A_5)		

The letters inserted in the table correspond with those in the skeleton table used to illustrate contingency. From the same table, with the help of the standard deviation, we may determine the correlation or concomitant variation between *measurable* attributes or capacities.

In finding an association coefficient we considered capacities, qualities, attributes, etc., qualitatively. We proceed, now, to deal with such as can be given definite numerical measures.

Let us suppose that we have a contingency table with small class intervals in which each 'array' of A's such as A_1, A_2, etc., is associated with only one value of B; i.e. each column has only one cell. This implies that every particular value of A is correlated with a particular value of B. If the subdivisions of A are sufficiently numerous, i.e. if the number of columns is indefinitely increased, and every column is reduced to a single cell, we should be justified in saying that every particular value of A determines or 'causes' a particular value of B. The test, therefore, of *causal relationship* or complete correlation between two variables is that each array shrinks to a single cell. All physical laws exemplify such complete correlation. Thus, if we were to construct a contingency table for two such variables as the temperature and volume of a gas, at a constant pressure, the above condition would be satisfied, i.e. for each temperature there would be one volume. Consequently we say that there is a causal relationship between the temperature and the volume, or that the temperature 'determines' the volume; but it would be better to say that the two are perfectly correlated.

The degree or intensity of the correspondence between two variables may be measured by the correlation ratio, or the correlation coefficient. Both these are based on the calculation of the standard deviation of the variables. We shall consider first the correlation ratio.

Let β_p denote any specific value of B in the array of B's in the column A_p; and $\bar{\beta}_p$ denote the mean value of this array. Then $(\beta_p - \bar{\beta}_p)$ is the deviation from the mean. Therefore, if S stands for the 'sum of all quantities like,'

$$\frac{S(\beta_p - \bar{\beta}_p)^2}{(A_p)} = \sigma_p^2 \text{ (where } \sigma \text{ is the standard deviation)}$$

Let

$$U = \frac{1}{N}\Big[S(\beta_1 - \bar{\beta}_1)^2 + S(\beta_2 - \bar{\beta}_2)^2 + \ldots . S(\beta_v - \bar{\beta}_v)^2 + \ldots .\Big]$$

$$= \frac{1}{N}\Big[(A_1)\,\sigma_1^2 + (A_2)\,\sigma_2^2 + \ldots\ldots\ldots . (A_p)\,\sigma_p^2 + \ldots\ldots\Big]$$

= Mean of the standard deviations squared of all the arrays, each array being 'weighted' with the frequency of the array.

We see that U can only be zero when there is complete correlation between A and B; for then there is only one value in each array, and consequently the sum of the squares of the deviations in each array is zero.

If A and B are entirely unrelated, or A does not in any way determine B, it is clear that the distribution of B's is similar in every array of A's and is similar to the distribution in the column of totals. In other words, every array is a reproduction in miniature of the whole universe of B's. It follows that, for complete independence:

$$\sigma_1^2 = \sigma_2^2 = \ldots\ldots\ldots\ldots = \sigma_p^2 = \ldots\ldots\ldots\ldots = \Sigma^2$$

Where Σ is standard deviation of the array of totals.

$$\text{Hence } U = \frac{1}{N} . \Sigma^2 [(A_1) + (A_2) + \ldots\ldots\ldots (A_p) + \ldots\ldots\ldots]$$

$$= \frac{1}{N} . N . \Sigma^2$$

$$= \Sigma^2$$

Thus the quantity $\frac{U}{\Sigma^2}$ takes every value from 0 to 1 as we pass from complete correlation to complete independence.

Now let us put $\eta = \sqrt{1 - \frac{U}{\Sigma^2}}$

For complete correlation $\eta = 1$ (for $U = 0$)
For complete independence $\eta = 0$ (for $U = \Sigma^2$).

For values between 0 and 1 there is limited association. Hence η is called the *correlation ratio,* and measures the degree of association or concomitant variation between quantitative characters; just as the coefficient of contingency does for qualitative classifications.

It can be shown by simple algebra (see Pearson's *Grammar of Science*, 3rd ed., p. 175) that

$$\eta = \frac{\text{standard deviation of the mean of the arrays}}{\text{standard deviation of the universe } (= \Sigma)}$$

In the numerator of this fraction each array should be weighted ' with the frequency of the array.

The probable error of a correlation ratio is $6745 \frac{1 - \eta^2}{\sqrt{n}}$

Note.—For each table there are, obviously, two correlation ratios accordingly as we deal with rows or columns.

Example.—Required to find the correlation ratio of the following table, which represents the mean intelligence quotients of 85 pairs of brothers and sisters.

Mean Intelligence Quotient.		*Younger Child.*					*Totals.*
		124	112	100	88	76	
Elder Child.	124	4	2	1	—	—	7
	112	1	7	5	2	—	15
	100	1	9	10	12	1	33
	88	—	2	11	7	1	21
	76	—	—	2	2	5	9
Totals ..		6	20	29	23	7	85

First we find the means of all the columns, and the squares of their standard deviations, using the method of p. 125 for each column. These figures are shown in the first two rows of the following table.

I.Q.	124	112	100	88	76	*Totals.*
Means	118	105·4	96·7	95·3	81·1	98·6
σ^2	84	93·2	128·1	84·3	76·9	167·4=Σ^2
Weights ..	6	20	29	23	7	85=N
Weight × σ^2 ..	504	1,864	3,715	1,939	538	8,560

The third row of the table called 'weights' is simply a repetition of the totals of the columns of the contingency table. The final row is obtained by multiplying the two previous rows: and its total is 8560.

Hence $$U = \frac{8560}{85} = 100{\cdot}7$$

$$\therefore \quad \eta = \sqrt{1 - \frac{100{\cdot}7}{167{\cdot}4}}$$

$$= {\cdot}63$$

The probable error is $\cdot 6745 \times \dfrac{1 - \eta^2}{\sqrt{n}}$

Hence the correlation ratio is $\cdot 63 \pm \cdot 04$

Note the following device for dealing with a set of grouped variables, as in the second column of Exercise 1, p. 143 (compare p. 125).

Class Limits (Mms.).	*Mid-Point.*	*Frequency* (*f*).	*Deviations* (δ).	($f.\delta$).	($f.\delta^2$).
133–135	134	3	−2	−6	12
136–138	137	5	−1	−5	5
139–141	140	4	0	—	—
142–144	143	1	+1	+1	1
145–147	146	1	+2	+2	4

Class interval=3 units; 14 $\Sigma(f.\delta)=-8,\ \Sigma(f.\delta^2)=22$

$$M=140-\frac{8}{14}\times 3=140-1\cdot 7;\quad s^2=\frac{22}{14}\times 3^2=14\cdot 1,\ \therefore \sigma^2=14\cdot 1-(1\cdot 7)^2.$$

Note the multiplication by 3 or 3^2 and the reason thereof.

Exercise 1.—Find the correlation ratio of the following measurements.

CEPHALIC MEASUREMENTS IN EGYPTIAN NATIVES (*Biometrika*, VOL. XIII., P. 22)

	Length of Head													
Breadth of Head	176–178	179–181	182–184	185–187	188–190	191–193	194–196	197–199	200–202	203–205	206–208	209–211	212–214	*Totals*
130–132			2	2	4									8
133–135	2	3	3	9	6	7	2	3						35
136–138	1	5	6	6	15	12	8	3						56
139–141	1	4	10	11	19	21	15	7	3	1				92
142–144		1	8	14	26	16	21	13	6	1	3			109
145–147	1	1	2	8	12	16	18	10	3					71
148–150			1	4	1	2	7	3	3	1	3			25
151–153			1	1		3	4	1	1					11
154–156					1	1				1				3
157–159													2	2
160–162							1							1
Totals	5	14	33	55	84	78	76	40	16	4	6	0	2	413

Answer: $\eta=\cdot 338\pm\cdot 03$

Exercise 2.—Find the correlation ratio for the following contingency table showing the mental ratios of brothers and sisters.

INHERITANCE OF INTELLIGENCE QUOTIENT IN SIBLINGS
(*Biometrika*, VOL. XII., P. 368)

Int. Quotient of Second Sibling	*Int. Quotient of First Sibling.*																		*Totals*
	50–55	55–60	60–65	65–70	70–75	75–80	80–85	85–90	90–95	95–100	100–105	105–110	110–115	115–120	120–125	125–130	130–135	135–140	
140–135											1								1
135–130										1				1					2
130–125										1	1			1					3
125–120								1			1		1						3
120–115							1		1							1	1		4
115–110							1	1	2	2	2	1	2		1				12
110–105			1						1	1	4	4	1						12
105–100						2		1	3		6	4	2		1	1		1	21
100–95				1			5		2	8		1	2			1	1		21
95–90		1		2	1		2	2	6	2	3	1	2	1					23
90–85	1		1		2	5	6		2		1		1		1				20
85–80				1	1	1	2	6	2	5			1	1					20
80–75			1	2		2	1	5			2								13
75–70			1	2	2		1	2	1										9
70–65			1		2	2	1		2	1									9
65–60				1	1	1		1				1							5
60–55									1										1
55–50								1											1
Totals	1	1	5	9	9	13	20	20	23	21	21	12	12	4	3	3	2	1	180

Answer: $\eta = \cdot 607 \pm \cdot 032$

$[r = \cdot 508 \pm \cdot 052]$

CHAPTER XVI

CORRELATION COEFFICIENT

We have seen that, in a contingency table, if the two variables are *independent* the distributions of all parallel arrays are similar to each other and to the distribution in the total universe of discourse. In such a case the means of every parallel array would be the same. Thus,

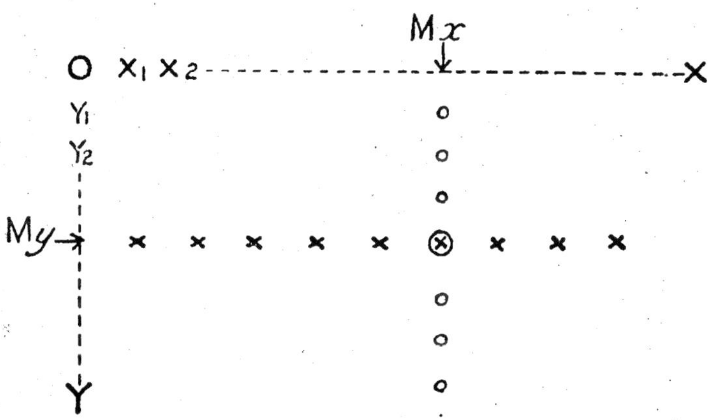

FIG. 17.

suppose the length of the head was entirely independent of the breadth in any particular race of people. If we selected different groups of persons whose head-lengths were between different assigned limits we should expect their mean head-breadths to be approximately the same; otherwise one would be in some way dependent on the other.

Suppose the diagram on p. 145 represents the skeleton of a contingency table, and M_x and M_y the position of the means of the variables X and Y respectively. The means of the separate rows and columns are shown by circles and crosses respectively. If the two variables are quite independent the means of the parallel arrays

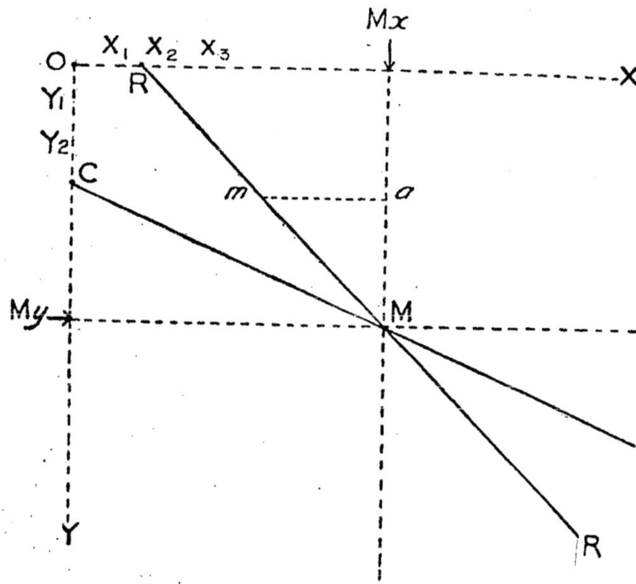

Fig. 18.

(rows and columns) must, in accordance with the above criterion, lie on two lines at right angles. Of course, this is an ideal case. In any real distribution the means would fluctuate more or less closely about these lines. When X and Y are completely dependent on each other, i.e. when each array shrinks to a single value, the variables all lie on a single line. It is as though the two lines of means had approached each other and finally coincided. Usually, however, where there is neither complete dependence nor independence the lines of the means of rows and columns stand at an acute angle to each other.

Let us suppose that the means of all the rows and column lie exactly on the straight lines RR and CC respectively.

Let M_y be the value of the mean of the Y variables, and let M_yM be drawn horizontally to cut RR in M. From the point M draw the vertical line MM_x; and let the tangent of the angle RMM_x be denoted by b_1. Let deviations from the lines M_xM and M_yM be denoted by x and y so that $b_1 = x/y$. Then for the row whose mean is at m and the number of variables is n, $\Sigma(x) = n.ma = n.b_1y$ (see p. 126). Therefore for all the rows together $\Sigma(x) = b_1 \Sigma(ny) = 0$, since $\Sigma(ny)$ is the sum of the deviations from the mean. Hence for the same reason M_x must be the mean of the variables X. Thus M is the mean of the whole table.

It is clearly a matter of indifference which variables are arranged in rows or columns.

Let the tangent of the angle of inclination of the line CC to the horizontal be b_2. Now the equations of the lines of means, namely RR and CC involve b_1 and b_2 and also the product of associated deviations, namely $\Sigma(xy)$. We shall proceed to find these equations. For any row

$$\Sigma(xy) = y\Sigma(x) = nb_1y^2$$

Hence, for the whole table (N being the total number of variables).

$$\Sigma\,(xy) = b_1\,\Sigma\,(ny^2) = b_1 N.\sigma_y^{\,2}$$

or

$$b_1 = \frac{\Sigma\,(xy)}{N\sigma_y^{\,2}} \quad \ldots\ldots\ldots\ldots\ldots\ldots\ldots (1)$$

Similarly

$$b_2 = \frac{\Sigma\,(xy)}{N\sigma_x^{\,2}} \quad \ldots\ldots\ldots\ldots\ldots\ldots\ldots (2)$$

Now, let

$$r = \frac{\Sigma\,(xy)}{N\sigma_x\sigma_y} \quad \ldots\ldots\ldots\ldots\ldots\ldots (3)$$

Then

$$b_1 = r\frac{\sigma_x}{\sigma_y} \text{ and } b_2 = r\frac{\sigma_y}{\sigma_x} \quad \ldots\ldots\ldots (4)$$

Hence the equations to RR and CC are:

$$x = r\frac{\sigma_x}{\sigma_y}.y \text{ and } y = r\frac{\sigma_y}{\sigma_x}.x \quad \ldots\ldots\ldots (5)$$

The number r whose value may be obtained from equation (3) is called the *coefficient of correlation.* The equation may be expressed in a variety of ways; for instance in terms of the variables X and Y themselves instead of the deviations x and y, by substituting

$$x = X - M_x \text{ and } y = Y - M_y$$

Again, since (by definition) $\Sigma x^2 = N\sigma_x^{\,2}$, and $\Sigma y^2 = N\sigma_y^{\,2}$, we have

$$r = \frac{\Sigma\,(xy)}{N\sigma_x\sigma_y} = \frac{\Sigma\,(xy)}{\sqrt{\Sigma x^2.\Sigma y^2}}$$

If the variables are independent $r=0$, for b_1 and b_2 are then zero, and X and Y are said to be uncorrelated. If the variables are completely correlated $r=1$. For, in this case, deviations of X are strictly proportional to deviations of Y; or $y=kx$.

Hence $$r=\frac{\Sigma(xy)}{\sqrt{\Sigma x^2.\Sigma y^2}}=\frac{k\Sigma x^2}{\sqrt{\Sigma x^2.k^2\Sigma x^2}}=1$$

If small values of x are completely correlated with large values of y, then $r=-1$, and the variables are said to be negatively correlated.

If $$r=\pm 1 \text{ then (by equation 5) } \frac{x}{y}=\pm\frac{\sigma_x}{\sigma_y}$$

in which case the lines RR and CC would coincide.

The quantities $b_1=r\frac{\sigma_x}{\sigma_y}$ and $b_2=r\frac{\sigma_y}{\sigma_x}$ are called the *coefficients of regression* of x on y and y on x respectively. The lines RR and CC are the *lines of regression*, and equations (5) are the corresponding regression equations.

Only when the regression is linear, or nearly so, should r be used as a measure of correspondence between the variables. When the concomitant variation is non-linear, i.e. when the means of arrays are not approximately on straight lines, the correspondence is measured by η, the correlation ratio. For linear regression $\eta=r$, otherwise η is greater than r.

The probable error of r is given by the expression

$$\cdot 6745 \frac{1 - r^2}{\sqrt{n}}$$

Thus its reliability is dependent on increasing n.

Method of Ranks.—Sometimes it is possible to assign an order or 'rank' to a number of individuals in different qualities or capacities without being able to give further numerical information concerning their relative merits. Thus a teacher might be able to range his pupils in order of merit for intelligence and industry respectively without being able to assign a numerical mark to intelligence or industry. In such a case

$$\frac{\Sigma(xy)}{N\sigma_x\sigma_y} \text{ becomes } 1 - \frac{\Sigma(d^2)}{\frac{1}{6}N(N^2 - 1)} = \rho$$

where d is the difference of rank for the same individual in the two different capacities. It can be shown that $\Sigma(d^2)$, or the sum of the differences in rank squared for the whole group, by chance, is given by $\frac{1}{6}N(N^2 - 1)$. If there were complete correlation there would, of course, be no difference of rank, in which case $\Sigma(d^2) = 0$ and consequently $\rho = 1$. If the sum of the differences in rank were due to chance, i.e. if there were no correlation, the second expression above $= 1 - 1$ and $\rho = 0$.

The formula for ρ is based on the dubious assumption that the differences between neighbouring ranks is the same at all parts of the scale, i.e. that the distribution is rectangular. If the distribution, however, is normal

$$r = 2 \sin \left(\frac{\pi}{6}\right) \rho$$

The probable error of r calculated by this formula is

$$\cdot 706 \frac{1 - r^2}{\sqrt{N}}$$

A simpler formula for correlation coefficients by the method of ranks is called the 'foot-rule.'

$$R = 1 - \frac{\Sigma (g)}{\frac{1}{6}(N^2 - 1)}$$

where $\Sigma(g)$ is the sum of the gains in rank of the same individuals in different capacities, and $\frac{1}{6}(N^2 - 1)$ is the number of gains due to chance. Hence $R = 0$ for complete absence of correlation, and 1 for complete correlation. It has been found that

$$r = 2 \cos \frac{\pi}{3} (1 - R) - 1$$

The probable error of $R = \frac{\cdot 43}{\sqrt{N}}$

The conception of '*partial correlation*' is frequently of value. Suppose we are considering three variables: (1) intelligence, (2) school marks, (3) age. The correlation between any pair of these may be denoted by r_{12}, r_{13}, and r_{23}. Yule has devised a formula for calculating the correlation between any two of the variates when the third is constant. Thus the correlation of (1) and (2) for constant value of (3) is

$$r_{12\cdot 3} = \frac{r_{12} - r_{13} \cdot r_{23}}{\sqrt{(1 - r^2_{13})(1 - r^2_{23})}}$$

Note carefully that even if r_{12} is zero, $r_{12\cdot 3}$ is not necessarily zero unless r_{13} or r_{23}, or both, are zero; and further, $r_{12\cdot 3}$ need not have the same sign as r_{12}.

We may use the correlation coefficient to get a measure of the reliability of any given tests. Suppose the same or closely similar tests are given to the same individuals on two successive occasions, or that the same tests are given to the same individuals by two different persons. Unless the ranking is very similar on both occasions the test has little validity. The correlation coefficient of the two sets of marks is called the *reliability coefficient.* Unless such coefficients are above ·6 the tests should be regarded with suspicion.

Suppose that r_{xy} is the coefficient of correlation between two sets of variates X and Y. If r_x is the reliability coefficient of X and r_y of Y, then we may correct r_{xy} as follows:

$$r_{\text{corr.}} = \frac{r_{xy}}{\sqrt{r_x \cdot r_y}}$$

This will, obviously, increase the 'raw coefficient' by an amount depending on the geometric mean of the reliability coefficients.

Example.—In order to illustrate the arithmetical processes, consider the marks X and Y gained in two tests by a number of individuals.

	X	Y	x	y	x^2	y^2	$x.y$	*Rank in* X	*Rank in* Y	*Difference in Rank* d	d^2
A	86	21	+26	+9	676	81	+234	1	3	−2	4
B	81	17	+21	+5	441	25	+105	2	4	−2	4
C	76	22	+16	+10	256	100	+160	3	2	1	1
D	73	15	+13	+3	169	9	+39	4	5	−1	1
E	66	24	+6	+12	36	144	+72	5	1	4	16
F	65	13	+5	+1	25	1	+5	6½	6½	0	0
G	65	12	+5	0	25	0	0	6½	8	−1½	2·25
H	61	10	+1	−2	1	4	−2	8	10	−2	4
J	55	13	−5	+1	25	1	−5	9	6½	2½	6·25
K	54	7	−6	−5	36	25	+30	10	11	−1	1
L	53	5	−7	−7	49	49	+49	11½	13	−1½	2·25
M	53	11	−7	−1	49	1	+7	11½	9	2½	6·25
N	49	6	−11	−6	121	36	+66	13	12	1	1
O	36	3	−24	−9	576	81	+216	14	14	0	0
P	27	1	−33	−11	1,089	121	+363	15	15	0	0

$N=15,\ M_x=60,\ M_y=12$ $\qquad \Sigma(g)=11\ \ \Sigma(d^2)=49$

$\sigma_x=15{\cdot}44, \sigma_y=6{\cdot}72,\ \Sigma(xy)=+1339$

$$r=\frac{\Sigma(xy)}{N\sigma_x\sigma_y}=\frac{1339}{15\times15{\cdot}44\times6{\cdot}72}=0{\cdot}86$$

$$\text{p.e.}=\frac{{\cdot}6745\,(1-r^2)}{\sqrt{N}}={\cdot}045$$

Hence $\qquad r={\cdot}86\pm{\cdot}045$

We may calculate the correlation by the method of ranks, using either $\Sigma(d^2)$ obtained from the last column, or $\Sigma(g)$ from the preceding column in which the gains in test Y are the positive differences in rank, and this equals the gains in test X, which are the negative quantities.

Thus

$$\rho = 1 - \frac{49}{\frac{1}{6}15(15^2 - 1)} = \cdot 91, \text{ whence } r = \cdot 92$$

$$R = 1 - \frac{11}{\frac{1}{6}(15^2 - 1)} = \cdot 71, \text{ whence } r = \cdot 91$$

It should be observed that whilst r calculated in this way is greater owing partly to the 'tied' cases, the p.e. is also greater.

We shall consider, finally, the graphical representation of the above calculations, which should be compared with the diagram on p. 146. The sets of marks or variables X and Y may be considered to form an incomplete contingency table, with several gaps.

By equation (5) we get $x = \cdot 86 \times \frac{15 \cdot 44}{6 \cdot 72} y$

but $\quad x = X - M_x = X - 60$

and $\quad y = Y - M_y = Y - 12$

whence $\quad X = 1 \cdot 97Y + 36 \cdot 36$

and $\quad Y = \cdot 37X - 10 \cdot 2$ (using the second equation)

Each individual such as A, etc., is now given his appropriate variables X and Y, which are plotted in the figure, as shown. By means of the above regression equations the regression lines RR and CC are drawn.

It will be seen that, since r is nearly unity, the lines almost coincide, and the points cluster round them.

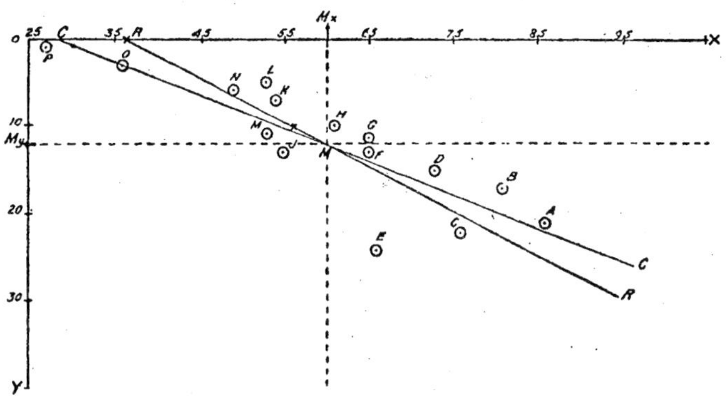

FIG. 19.—SHOWING HOW THE VARIABLES CLUSTER ROUND THE REGRESSION LINES

Exercise 1.—Find the correlation-coefficient and the regression equations for the corresponding values of X and Y. Plot the values in a diagram and draw the lines of regression.

X	190	197	196	191	195	192	194	196	199	190	191	196	195
Y	140	150	144	140	144	148	146	152	146	142	143	145	145

Answer: $r = 0{\cdot}63$.

Exercise 2.—The following table shows the mean mental ratio and the corresponding mean educational ratio of 689 school children. Find r.

Mental ratio:								
67	72	77	82	87	92	97	102	107
Educational ratio:								
62	70·3	74·5	83	90·4	95	97·8	99·5	102·5

Mental ratio:

112 117 122 127 132 137 142 147 152

Educational ratio:

105·2 109·3 108·2 112 119·9 108·7 113·7 117 122

Answer: ·94 ± ·18

Exercise 3.—Find the coefficients of contingency and correlation for the following table showing the intelligence quotients of 85 pairs of brothers and sisters.

Intelligence Quotient		*Younger Child*				*Totals*
	118 +	117 to 106	105 to 94	93 to 82	81 –	
Elder Child 118 +	4	2	1			7
117–106	1	7	5	2		15
105–94	1	9	10	12	1	33
93–82		2	11	7	1	21
81–			2	2	5	9
Total	6	20	29	23	7	85

Answer: C = ·67. $r = 0·675 \pm ·04$.

References for Further Reading

An Introduction to the Theory of Statistics. By G. U. Yule. Griffin and Co., Ltd.

The best and clearest practical exposition, using only elementary algebra.

The Grammar of Science. Chs. IV. and V. By K. Pearson. A. and C. Black.

Very good theoretical discussion of measures of relationship.

The Principles of Science. Chs. XVI. and XVII. 3rd edition. By W. S. Jevons. Macmillan and Co.

Deals with first principles in an interesting way.

The Essentials of Mental Measurement. By Brown and Thomson. Cambridge University Press.

An advanced textbook, using higher mathematics.

APPENDICES

APPENDIX I

A.—SUITS OF ARMOUR

1

2

4

3

B.—DIAGRAMS OF ARMOUR

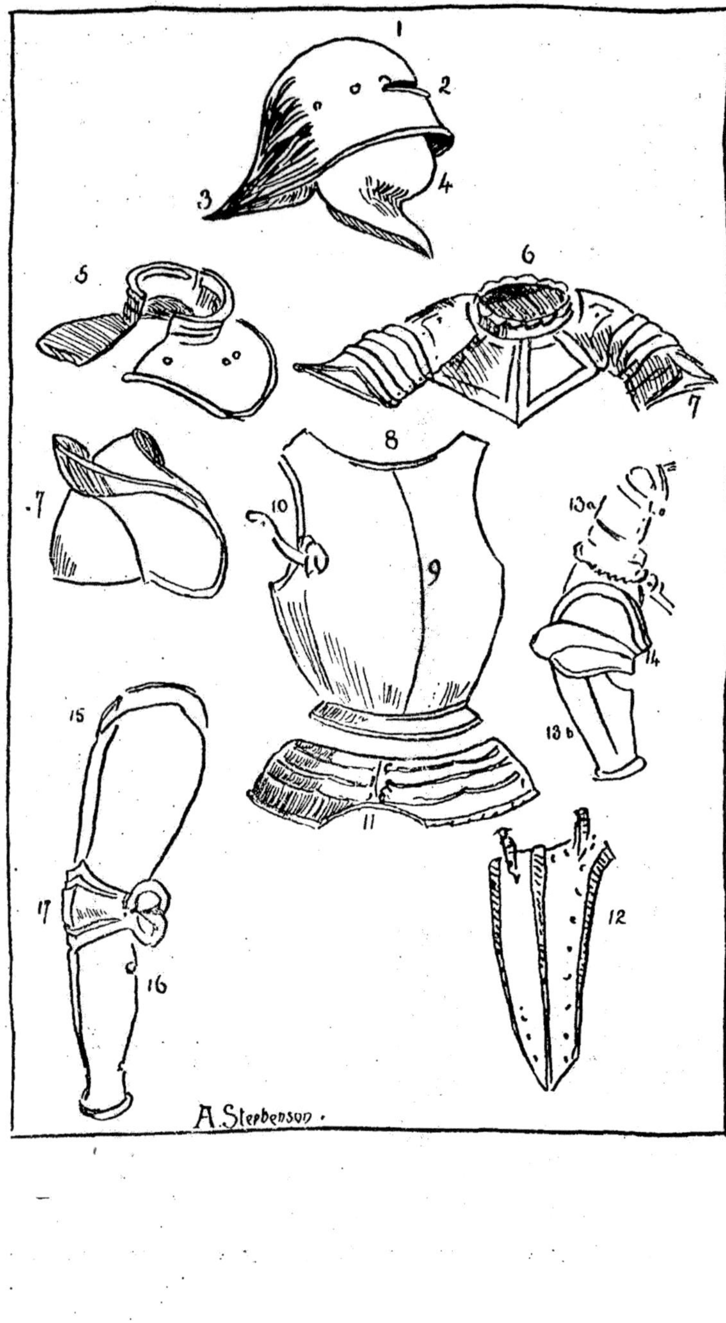

C.—LECTURE ON ARMOUR

A gradual progress is evident in the improvement of arms from the earliest times. Starting from the tenth century we are able to follow step by step the gradual change in defensive armour. The mail shirt remained in use for over five hundred years, and was replaced by complete plate armour only after a transition period in which coats of mail partly composed of plates of iron were used. The armour of the sixteenth century had beautiful flutings called *Milanaise,* and in the second half of this century was adorned with chased engravings.

Our pictures are concerned with the perfected plate armour showing some traces of the old coats of mail as vestiges of the earlier covering.

The casque or helmet was of diverse shapes and of great antiquity, but the real bowl-shaped helm, the *salade,* only came into use in the fifteenth century. This sometimes had a *neck guard* at the back and had a moveable or fixed *visor* or sight piece, which however was usually so short (end of nose) that a *beaver*, or chin piece, was

---

Key to figures opposite.

1. Salade.	7. Pauldrons.	13*a*. Upper arm guard.
2. Vizor.	8. Cuirass.	13*b*. Lower arm guard.
3. Neck guard.	9. Ridge.	14. Elbow piece.
4. Beaver.	10. Lance rest.	15. Cuisse.
5. Neck collar.	11. Great brayette.	16. Greaves.
6. Gorget.	12. Tasset.	17. Knee plate.

necessary to guard the chin, neck and mouth. Later came a rounded helmet or *armet*, the crown of which was sometimes crested and sometimes the chin piece and gorget were fastened to it.

The neck collar, made of leather, which supported the rest of the body armour and lying underneath (therefore never seen) supported the *gorget*, or throat guard, sometimes with *pauldrons*, or shoulder plates, attached. Often the pauldron was a separate part.

Below was the *cuirass*, or breast plate, which protected the chest and was often made with a *prominent ridge*. This had usually a *lance rest*, which was placed on the right of the breast plate and was used to support the lance, when on horseback.

Below the breast plate was the waist piece or *brayette*, that part of the armour which guarded the abdomen. It was composed of steel plates and usually ended in *tassets*, designed to protect the upper part of the thighs, and strapped with thongs to the brayette.

The arms were protected by the *arm guards*, composed of upper and lower armplates joined together by the *elbow piece*, which sometimes had prominent wings.

The legs were guarded by the *cuisses* on thighs, and the *greaves* on the shins, joined by the *knee plate*, sometimes with wings.

In addition there were *gauntlets*, with or without separately articulated fingers; and the armed shoes or *solerets*, sometimes with long points.

APPENDIX II

CONTINUOUS TEXTS

A

Whilerevolutionshavetakenplaceallaroundusourgovernmenthas
neveroncebeensubvertedbyviolenceduringmorethanahundredyears
therehasbeeninourislandnotumultofsufficientimportancetobecalledan
insurrectionnorhasthelawbeenoncebornedowneitherbypopularfuryor
byregaltyrannypubliccredithasbeenheldsacredtheadministrationofjus
ticehasbeenpureevenintimeswhichmightbyenglishmenbejustlycalled
eviltimeswehaveenjoyedwhatalmosteveryothernationintheworld
wouldhaveconsideredasanamplemeasureofcivilandreligiousfreedom
everymanhasfeltentireconfidencethatthestatewouldprotecthiminthe
possessionofwhathadbeenearnedbyhisdiligenceandhoardedbyhisselfde
nialunderthebenignantinfluenceofpeaceandlibertysciencehasflourish
edandhasbeenappliedtopracticalpurposesonascaleneverbeforeknown
theconsequenceisthatachangetowhichthehistoryoftheoldworldfur
nishesnoparallelhastakenplaceinourcountrycouldtheenglandof1685be
bysomemagicalprocesssetbeforeoureyesweshouldnotknowoneland
scapeinahundredoronebuildingintenthousandthecountrygentleman
wouldnotrecognizehisownfieldstheinhabitantofthetownwouldnotrecog
nizehisownstreeteverythinghasbeenchangedbutthegreatfeaturesofna
tureandafewmassiveanddurableworksofhumanartwemightfindout
snowdonandwindermerethecheddarcliffsandbeachyheadwemightfind
outhereandthereanormanminsteroracastlewhichwitnessedthewarsof
therosesbutwithsuchrareexceptionseverythingwouldbestrangetous
manythousandsofsquaremileswhicharenowrichcornlandandmeadows
intersectedbygreenhedgerowsanddottedwithvillagesandpleasant
countryseatswouldappearasmoorsovergrownwithfurzeorfensabandon
edtowildducksweshouldseestragglinghutsbuiltofwoodandcoveredwith
thatchwherewenowseemanufacturingtownsandseaportsrenownedto
thefarthestendsoftheworldthecapitalitselfwouldshrinktodimensions
notmuchexceedingthoseofitspresentsuburbonthesouthofthethames
notlessstrangetouswouldbethegarbandmannersofthepeoplethefurni
tureandtheequipagestheinterioroftheshopsanddwellingssuchachange
inthestateofanationseemstobeatleastaswellentitledtothenoticeofa
historianasanychangeofthedynastyorofthreministry

B

Oneofthefirstobjectsofanenquirerwhowishestoformacorrectnotionof
thestateofacommunityatagiventimemustbetoascertainofhowmanyper
sonsthatcommunitythenconsistedunfortunatelythepopulationofeng
landin1685cannotbeascertainedwithperfectaccuracyfornogreatstate
hadthenadoptedthewisecourseofperiodicallynumberingthepeopleall
menwerelefttoconjectureforthemselvesandastheygenerallyconjectur
edwithoutexaminingfactsandundertheinfluenceofstrongpassionsand
prejudicestheirguesseswereoftenludicrouslyabsurdevenintelligent
londonersordinarilytalkedoflondonascontainingseveralmillionsofsouls
itwasconfidentlyassertedbymanythatduringthethirtyfiveyearswhich
hadelapsedbetweentheaccessionofcharlesthefirstandtherestorationthe
populationofthecityhadincreasedbytwomillionsevenwhiletheravages
oftheplagueandfirewererecentitwasthefashiontosaythatthecapitalstill
hadamillionandahalfofinhabitantssomepersonsdisgustedbytheseexag
gerationsranviolentlyintotheoppositeextremethusamanofundoubted
partsandlearningstrenuouslymaintainedthattherewereonlytwomil
lionsofhumanbeingsinenglandscotlandandirelandtakentogetherweare
nothoweverleftwithoutthemeansofcorrectingthewildblundersinto
whichsomemindswerehurriedbynationalvanityandothersbyamorbid
loveofparadoxthereareextantthreecomputationswhichseemtobeen
titledtopeculiarattentiontheyareentirelyindependentofeachotherthey
proceedondifferentprinciplesandyetthereislittledifferenceintheresults
oneofthesecomputationswasmadeintheyear1696byapoliticalarithme
ticianofgreatacutenessandjudgmentthebasisofhiscalculationswasthe
numberofhousesreturnedin1690bytheofficerswhomadethelastcollec
tionofthehearthmoneytheconclusionatwhichhearrivedwasthatthe
populationofenglandwasnearlyfivemillionsandahalfaboutthesametime
kingwilliamthethirdwasdesiroustoascertainthecomparativestrengthof
thereligioussectsintowhichthecommunitywasdividedanenquirywas
institutedandreportswerelaidbeforehimfromallthediocesesoftherealm
accordingtothesereportsthenumberofhisenglishsubjectsmusthavebeen
aboutfivemilliontwohundredthousand

C

Lastlyinourowndaysanactuaryofeminentskillsubjectedtheancient
parochialregistersofbaptismsmarriagesandburialstoallthetestswhich
themodernimprovementsinstatisticalscienceenabledhimtoapplyhis
opinionwasthatatthecloseoftheseventeenthcenturythepopulationof
englandwasalittleunderfivemilliontwohundredthousandsoulsofthese
threeestimatesframedwithoutconcertbydifferentpersonsfromdifferent
setsofmaterialsthehighestdoesnotexceedthelowestbyonetwelfthwe
maythereforewithconfidencepronouncethatwhenjamesthesecond
reignedenglandcontainedbetweenfivemillionandfivemillionfivehun
dredthousandinhabitantsontheveryhighestsuppositionshethenhadless
thanonethirdofherpresentpopulationandlessthanthreetimesthepopula
tionwhichisnowcollectedinhergiganticcapitaltheincreaseofthepeople
hasbeengreatineverypartofthekingdombutgenerallymuchgreaterinthe
northernthaninthesouthernshiresintruthalargepartofthecountrybe
yondtrentwasdowntotheeighteenthcenturyinastateofbarbarismphysi
calandmoralcauseshadconcurredtopreventcivilizationfromspreadingto
thatregiontheairwasinclementthesoilwasgenerallysuchasrequiredskil
fulandindustriouscultivationandtherecouldbelittleskillorindustryina
tractwhichwasoftenthetheatreofwarandwhichevenwhentherewasnom
inalpeacewasconstantlydesolatedbybandsofscottishmaraudersbefore
theunionofthetwobritishcrownsandlongafterthatuniontherewasas
greatadifferencebetweenmiddlesexandnorthumberlandastherenowis
betweenmassachusettsandthesettlementsofthosesquatterswhofartothe
westofthemississippiadministerarudejusticewiththerifleandthedagger
inthereignofcharlesthesecondthetracesleftbyagesofslaughterandpillage
weredistinctlyperceptiblemanymilessouthofthetweedinthefaceofthe
countryandinthelawlessmannersofthepeopletherewasstillalargeclassof
mosstrooperswhosecallingwastoplunderdwellingsandtodriveawaywho
leherdsofcattleitwasfoundnecessarysoonaftertherestorationtoenact
lawsofgreatseverityforthepreventionoftheseoutragesthemagistratesof
northumberlandandcumberlandwereauthorizedtoraisebandsofarmed
menforthedefenceofpropertyandorderandprovisionwasmadeformeet
ingtheexpenseoftheseleviesbylocaltaxationtheparisheswererequiredto
keepbloodhoundsforthepurposeofhuntingthefreebootersmanyoldmen
whowerelivinginthemiddleoftheeighteenthcenturycouldwellremember
thetimewhenthoseferociousdogswerecommonyetevenwithsuchauxili
ariesitwasoftenfoundimpossibletotracktherobberstotheirretreats
amongthehillsandmorasses

D

Ofthetaxationwecanspeakwithmoreconfidenceandprecisionthanof thepopulationtherevenueofenglandwhencharlesthesecondd iedwas smallwhencomparedwiththeresourceswhichsheeventhenpossessedor withthesumswhichwereraisedbythegovernmentsoftheneighbouring countriesithadfromthetimeoftherestorationbeenalmostconstantlyin creasingyetitwaslittlemorethanthreefourthsoftherevenueoftheunited provincesandwashardlyonefifthoftherevenueoffrancethemostimpor tantheadofreceiptwastheexcisewhichinthelastyearofthereignofcharles producedfivehundredandeightyfivethousandpoundsclearofalldeduc tionsthenetproceedsofthecustomsamountedinthesameyeartofive hundredandthirtythousandpoundstheseburdensdidnotlieveryheavy onthenationthetaxonchimneysthoughlessproductivecalledforthfar loudermurmursthediscontentexcitedbydirectimpostsisindeedalmost alwaysoutofproportiontothequantityofmoneywhichtheybringintothe exchequerandthetaxonchimneyswasevenamongdirectimpostspecu liarlyodiousforitcouldbeleviedonlybymeansofdomiciliaryvisitsandof suchvisitstheenglishhavealwaysbeenimpatienttoadegreewhichthe peopleofothercountriescanbutfaintlyconceivethepoorerhouseholders werefrequentlyunabletopaytheirhearthmoneytothedaywhenthishap penedtheirfurniturewasdistrainedwithoutmercyforthetaxwasfarmed andafarmeroftaxesisofallcreditorsproverbiallythemostrapaciousthe collectorswereloudlyaccusedofperformingtheirunpopulardutywith harshnessandinsolenceitwassaidthatassoonastheyappearedatthethres holdofacottagethechildrenbegantowailandtheoldwomenrantohide theirearthenwarenaythesinglebedofapoorfamilyhadsometimesbeen carriedawayandsoldthenetannualreceiptfromthistaxwastwohundred thousandpoundswhentothethreegreatsourcesofincomewhichhavebeen mentionedweaddtheroyaldomainsthenfarmoreextensivethanatpre sentthefirstfruitsandtenthswhichhadnotyetbeensurrenderedtothe churchtheduchiesofcornwallandlancastertheforfeituresandthefineswe shallfindthatthewholeannualrevenueofthecrownmaybefairlyestimated ataboutfourteenhundredthousandpoundsofthisrevenuepartwashere ditarytheresthadbeengrantedtocharlesforlifeandhewasatlibertytolay outthewholeexactlyashethoughtfitwhateverhecouldsavebyretrench ingfromtheexpenditureofthepublicdepartmentswasanadditiontohis privypurseofthepostofficemorewillhereafterbesaidtheprofitsofthat establishmenthadbeenappropriatedbyparliamenttothedukeofyork

E

Inourislandonthecontraryitwaspossibletolivelongandtotravelfar
withoutbeingonceremindedbyanymartialsightorsoundthatthedefence
ofnationshadbecomeascienceandacallingthemajorityofenglishmen
whowereundertwentyfiveyearsofagehadprobablyneverseenacompany
ofregularsoldiersofthecitieswhichinthecivilwarhadvaliantlyrepelled
hostilearmiesscarcelyonewasnowcapableofsustainingasiegethegates
stoodopennightanddaytheditchesweredrytherampartshadbeensuffer
edtofallintodecayorwererepairedonlythatthetownsfolkmighthavea
pleasantwalkonsummereveningsoftheoldbaronialkeepsmanyhadbeen
shatteredbythecannonoffairfaxandcromwellandlayinheapsofruinover
grownwithivythosewhichremainedhadlosttheirmartialcharacterand
werenowruralpalacesofthearistocracythemoatswereturnedintopre
servesofcarpandpikethemoundswereplantedwithfragrantshrubs
throughwhichspiralwalksranuptosummerhousesadornedwithmirrors
andpaintingsonthecapesoftheseacoastandonmanyinlandhillswerestill
seentallpostssurmountedbybarrelsoncethosebarrelshadbeenfilledwith
pitchwatchmenhadbeensetroundtheminseasonsofdangerandwithina
fewhoursafteraspanishsailhadbeendiscoveredinthechanneloraftera
thousandscottishmosstroopershadcrossedthetweedthesignalfireswere
blazingfiftymilesoffandwholecountieswererisinginarmsbutmanyyears
hadnowelapsedsincethebeaconshadbeenlightedandtheywereregarded
ratherascuriousrelicsofancientmannersthanaspartsofamachinerynecces
saryforthesafetyofthestatetheonlyarmywhichthelawrecognizedwasthe
militiathatforcehadbeenremodelledbytwoactsofparliamentpassed
shortlyaftertherestorationeverymanwhopossessedfivehundredpounds
ayearderivedfromlandorsixthousandpoundsofpersonalestatewas
boundtoprovideequipandpayathisownchargeonehorsemaneveryman
whohadfiftypoundsayearderivedfromlandorsixhundredpoundsofper
sonalestatewaschargedinlikemannerwithonepikemanormusketeer
smallerproprietorswerejoinedtogetherinakindofsocietyforwhichourlan
guagedoesnotaffordaspecialnameandeachsocietywasrequiredtofurnish
accordingtoitsmeansahorsesoldieroralootsoldierthewholenumberof
cavalryandinfantrythusmaintainedwaspopularlyestimatedatahun
dredandthirtythousandmenthekingwasbytheancientconstitutionofthe
realmandbytherecentandsolemnacknowledgmentofbothhousesofpar
liamentthesolecaptaingeneralofthislargeforcethelordslieutenantsand
theirdeputiesheldthecommandunderhimandappointedmeetingsfor
drillingandinspectionthetimeoccupiedbysuchmeetingshoweverwasnot
toexceedfourteendaysinoneyearthejusticesofthepeacewereauthorized
toinflictslightpenaltiesforbreachesofdisciplineoftheordinarycostnopart
waspaidbythecrownbutwhenthetrainbandswerecalledoutagainstan
enemytheirsubsistencebecameachargeonthegeneralrevenueofthestate
andtheyweresubjecttotheutmostrigourofmartiallaw

F

Inonerespectitmustbeadmittedthattheprogressofcivilizationhasdi
minishedthephysicalcomfortsofaportionofthepoorestclassithasalready
beenmentionedthatbeforetherevolutionmanythousandsofsquaremiles
nowenclosedandcultivatedweremarshforestandheathofthiswildland
muchwasbylawcommonandmuchofwhatwasnotcommonbylawwas
worthsolittlethattheproprietorssufferedittobecommoninfactinsucha
tractsquattersandtrespasserswereetoleratedtoanextentnowunknown
thepeasantwhodwelttherecouldatlittleornochargeprocureoccasionally
somepalatableadditiontohishardfareandprovidehimselfwithfuelforthe
winterhekeptaflockofgeeseonwhatisnowanorchardrichwithappleblos
somshesnaredwildfowlonthefenwhichhaslongsincebeendrainedand
dividedintocornfieldsandturnipfieldshecutturfamongthefurzebushes
onthemoorwhichisnowameadowbrightwithcloverandrenownedfor
butterandcheesetheprogressofagricultureandtheincreaseofpopulation
necessarilydeprivedhimoftheseprivilegesbutagainstthisdisadvantage
alonglistofadvantagesistobesetoffoftheblessingswhichcivilizationand
philosophybringwiththemalargeproportioniscommontoallranksand
wouldifwithdrawnbemissedaspainfullybythelabourerasbythepeerthe
marketplacewhichtherusticcannowreachwithhiscartinanhourwasa
hundredandsixtyyearsagoadaysjourneyfromhimthestreetwhichnow
affordstotheartisanduringthewholenightasecureaconvenientandabril
liantlylightedwalkwasahundredandsixtyyearsagosodarkaftersunset
thathewouldnothavebeenabletoseehishandsoillpavedthathewould
haverunconstantriskofbreakinghisneckandsoillwatchedthathewould
havebeeninimminentdangerofbeingknockeddownandplunderedofhis
smallearningseverybricklayerwhofallsfromascaffoldeverysweeperofa
crossingwhoisrunoverbyacarriagemaynowhavehiswoundsdressedand
hislimbssetwithaskillsuchasahundredandsixtyyearsagoallthewealthof
agreatlordorofamerchantprincecouldnothavepurchasedsomefrightful
diseaseshavebeenextirpatedbyscienceandsomehavebeenbanishedby
policethetermofhumanlifehasbeenlengthenedoverthewholekingdom
andespeciallyinthetownstheyear1685wasnotaccountedsicklyyetinthe
year1685morethanoneintwentythreeoftheinhabitantsofthecapitaldied
atpresentonlyoneinhabitantofthecapitalinfortydiesannuallythediffer
enceinsalubritybetweenthelondonofthenineteenthcenturyandthe
londonoftheseventeenthcenturyisveryfargreaterthanthedifference
betweenlondoninanordinaryyearandlondoninayearofcholerastillmore
importantisthebenefitwhichallordersofsocietyandespeciallythelower
ordershavederivedfromthemollifyinginfluenceofcivilizationonthe
nationalcharacterthegroundworkofthatcharacterhasindeedbeenthe
samethroughmanygenerationsinthesenseinwhichthegroundworkofthe
characterofanindividualmaybesaidtobethesamewhenheisarudeand
thoughtlessschoolboyandwhenheisarefinedandaccomplishedman

APPENDIX III

ALPHABETS FOR THE CURVE OF ATTAINMENT

1. a r u y b q v z c p s x d o t w e m i k f n h l g j
2. r y q z p x o w m k n l j a u b v c s d t e i f h g
3. u q c x t m f l a y v p d w i n g r b z s o e k h j
4. j g l h n f k i m e w t o d x s p c z v q b y u r a
5. g h f i e t d s c v b u a j l n k m w o x p z q y r
6. j h k e o s z b r g n i w d p v y a l f m t x c q u
7. w d i p v n y a r b l f z s m t o e x c k h q u j g
8. a j g r u l h y b n f q v k i z c m e p s w t o x d
9. g r y h f q z i e p x t d o w s c m k v b n l u j a
10. j u q h k c x e o t m s z f l b r a y g n v p i d w

APPENDIX IV

SUGGESTION PICTURES

1

2

3

4

5

6

APPENDIX V

REASONING TESTS

Solutions to Reasoning Tests

The following may be regarded as typical correct answers earning 1 mark, but any other method of reasoning which secures the same result is given a full mark.

(1) Iridescence is due to the light reflected and refracted from the form of the surface and not to the nature of the substance.

(2) No. Because there is an appreciable chance that the sets of 23 and 14 are mutually exclusive.

(3) Let T be the observed time of the eclipse, *t* the calculated time. The argument runs thus·

If Newton's laws are true $t = T$;
but $t = T$,

$\therefore$ the laws are true.

This is formally invalid since we cannot infer the truth of the antecedent for the truth of the consequent.

(4) No member of the University in 1920 knew both Russian and French. For, if he did, he would be found

in X College or in some other college. But he is not in X College by the first premiss, nor in any other by the second.

(5) The term 'desirable' is not analogous in meaning to visible or any sense experience. It means worthy of desire, or ought to be desired by a rational being.

(6) Let *f* be a member of the financial committee.

g	,,	,,	,,	general	,,
l	,,	,,	,,	library	,,

Rule 1 means all *f* are *g*.
Rule 2 means if any *l* is *g*, that *l* is *f*.
Rule 3 means No. *l* is *f*.

From rules 2 and 3, it follows that no *l* is *g*. Hence the rules means (*a*) All *f* are *g*, (*b*) no *l* is *g*, (*c*) no *l* is *f*. But (*c*) can be inferred from (*a*) and (*b*). Hence only (*a*) and (*b*) are necessary rules. Therefore Rule (2) from "unless he be——" and Rule (3) are superfluous.

(7) Begs the question. We have experience of past futures, but not of future futures. The real point is "Will future futures resemble past times which were once future?" This cannot be answered by reference to the past futures alone. We still need a principle whereby we may argue from 'past futures' to 'future futures.'

(8) Unsound. The 'general happiness' is not, by this argument, a good to any person or aggregate of persons. An aggregate of happy persons is not neces-

sarily a happy community. There are also implicit assumptions which are questionable, namely, that desired is equivalent to desirable, that the 'General happiness' cannot conflict with individual happiness, and that individual goods can be aggregated to a 'general good.'

Hints for Marking.—Question (1): ½ mark for merely saying that the phenomenon is not due to the substance; or for merely saying it is due to light.

Question (2): ½ mark for saying that the sum of nervous and mentally deficient children is less than the number examined.

Question (3): 1 mark for saying that coincidence of observed and calculated times might be due to other laws; 1 mark for saying that every correctly calculated eclipse increases the probability of the laws; ½ mark for the statement that the coincidence might be due to chance; ½ for the statement that it is possible for 2 formulæ to give similar results, within limits.

Question (5): 1 mark for saying desire is not a sense and therefore the analogy is wrong, 1 for desire depends on emotion and will which are fallible, 1 for it is possible for something to be desirable without people desiring it or even knowing it; ½ if the person suspects a difference between desirable and visible, without stating it.

Question (6): ½ for stating either that Rule 3 is superfluous or latter part of rule (2).

Question (7): ½ mark for stating that past and future

are exclusive terms; ½ for stating that future is never experienced, only the past.

Question (8): 1 mark for we cannot aggregate individual happiness since they are incommensurable; ½ for good of whole is not necessarily the good of all the individuals; ½ for individual desires or happiness may conflict.

APPENDIX VI

KNOWLEDGE TESTS

Hints for Marking

Literature

1. Must state 2 out of 3 plays.
2. Must state Dickens; and character of the man.
6. Must state Sheridan and blunders.

Philosophy

2. Must state at least 1 name and the theory; or 2 names, or the theory correctly.
3. Two of the following must be stated, (*a*) offspring differ from parents in indefinite ways, (*b*) natural selection favours survival of those fitted for environment, (*c*) new species arise from the struggle.
4. Any one theory may be accepted.

History

4. Allow 10 years error.

Geography

2. Must state fairly precise position.
3. Must state that temperatures or mean temperatures occur at same time or period.

Politics

2. Allow 10 years error.
4. Must state doctrines; or names of Bright and Cobden.

Science

1. Two properties must be given correctly.
4. Correct if it is defined as the unit of electricity.

Mythology

1. Should state at least 2 of the following: (*a*) he stole fire from heaven, (*b*) was imprisoned on a rock, (*c*) vulture devoured his liver.

Medicine

4. Two must be given including the last out of: Vomiting, lumbar pains, pustular eruption.

Synonyms

The differences given in Webster must be regarded as final in this section.

INDEX TO EXPERIMENTS

GENERAL INDEX